The Barnabas Quest

The Journey Along a Lonely and Twisting Road

James Perry

The Barnabas Quest

Copyright © 2020 by James Perry

All rights reserved. No part of this book may be reproduced or transmitted in any form or by any means without written permission of the author.

ISBN 9781733454063

Book Dedication - Steve Sellers

A servant of the Lord!

A man of faith and prayer!

A friend to and for the friendless!

Faithfully represented
Alabama Baptist Home for Children
and Family Ministry

Retired from his leadership position
January 2021

A man who epitomizes what it means to be
a Biblical Barnabas!

I am grateful to the lord for Steve –
his prayers and encouragement
sustained me when I needed a Barnabas
during a low point in my life!

May his tribe increase!

Table of Contents

Introduction 1
1. The Path We Take 5
2. Disheartened 11
3. Observation 17
4. Intercession 23
5. Availability 29
6. Readiness 35
7. Willingness 41
8. Teachability 47
9. Scriptualization 53
10. Candidates 59
11. Inexcusable 65
12. Underestimation 73
13. Prayerfulness 79
14. Quitting 85
15. Action 89
16. Overcoming 95
17. Resolute 103
18. Frustration 107
19 Eagerness 113
20. Equipped 119

21. Teachability	127
22. Shadows	133
23. Breakthrough	139
24. Influencers	145
25. Aspiration	151
Epilogue	157

Introduction

Anyone who sets out to write a book has a reason for doing so. A man named Barnabas triggered the focus and title of the book and the content that would be part of the chronicle. We first learn about Barnabas in Acts 4:36-37 (NASB):

Now Joseph, a Levite of Cyprian birth, who was also called Barnabas by the apostles (which translated means Son of Encouragement), and who owned a tract of land, sold it and brought the money and laid it at the apostles' feet.

We don't read too much more about Barnabas in the New Testament. He is mentioned in Acts 9 where he interceded in behalf of the recent convert, Saul. We read about him once again in Acts 15 when he becomes engaged in an emotional confrontation with this same Saul (known as Paul) regarding his nephew John Mark.

The title of this book, The Barnabas Quest, is occasioned by a brief phrase that occurs in Acts 9. There are interesting phrases using the conjunction "but" that occur within Acts 9:

(Vs. 1) "But Saul";
(Vs. 13) "But Ananias"
(Vs. 15) "But the Lord"
(Vs. 24) "But their plot"; and then,
(Vs. 27) "But Barnabas"

Barnabas played a significant role in the life of Saul from Tarsus after his conversion. We see within the context of Acts

9:27 that Barnabas vouched for Saul which allowed him to be accepted as a true convert. The NASB translates verses 26-27,

> When he (Saul) came to Jerusalem, he was trying to associate with the disciples; but they were all afraid of him, not believing that he was a disciple. But Barnabas took hold of him and brought him to the apostles and described to them how he had seen the Lord on the road, and that He had talked to him, and how at Damascus he had spoken out boldly in the name of Jesus.

Why did just one person, Barnabas, rise to the occasion and speak on behalf and in defense of Saul? Why is it that no one else stood up or spoke up on behalf of Saul? Was "being afraid" a justifiable reason for not accepting the work of Jesus Christ in the life and focus of Saul? Do we react similarly in the Church today when someone tries to become part of "our gathering" and "our assembly"? Do we have any who are like Barnabas in our midst? Is there anyone willing to risk one's reputation and integrity on behalf of the one of whom all others are afraid?

The words of Barnabas were timely, trustworthy, affirmative and confirmed that Saul was a new creature in Christ. As such, Saul was to be trusted and heard because the Lord had brought about a miraculous transformation in this one who had been such a terrorist to the believers and the churches. Barnabas was willing to risk his own reputation in

Introduction

his representation to the Jewish believers that Saul should be received, welcomed and accepted. He affirmed that Saul was alright and the people needed to trust both the counsel of Barnabas and the message that would be shared by Saul.

Acts 15 takes note that Saul/Paul and Barnabas had gone about proclaiming the Gospel and establishing churches. The regard of the Jerusalem Council indicates the esteem and appreciation with which they were held. Acts 15:25-26, "It has seemed good to us, having come to one accord, to choose men and send them to you with our beloved Barnabas and Paul, men who have risked their lives for the name of our Lord Jesus Christ." These words are an outstanding recognition of the courage and boldness of two men who were willing to do the will of God regardless of any personal cost. In a following Chapter, Barnabas and his role in the lives of others will be highlighted. While there is not much written about his family and background, we noted the brief statement made about him. Acts 4:36 describes him as a man of sacrifice and commitment who was willing to risk everything if only he could reach a person or groups of people for Jesus Christ and the Gospel.

Based on this description, who is an identifiable Barnabas? Is it someone young, or one who is older? Does encouragement and/or consolation require one to be of a certain age or education level? If you were a member in good standing of a particular church and you had a special or pressing need, is there someone – anyone – you could confidently seek out to pray with you or to intercede in your behalf? If there was a Saul of Tarsus who had been converted and passed your way, would you risk your reputation and integrity to see to it that he was accepted by others? Would your particular church view you as a rabble-rouser if you attempted to do so? Would that have any significant influence in terms of you being like Barnabas?

In The Barnabas Quest, each of us will have to be completely transparent before the Lord and examine whether we are ready and willing to be and do whatever is required of us by Him in the implementation of Romans 15:7 to: "Accept one another, then, just as Christ accepted you, in order to bring praise to God" (NIV)? Will you be or become a Barnabas (an encourager and consoler) for Jesus Christ?

1. The Path We Take

In 1920, Robert Frost wrote a poem, "The Road Not Taken." A couple of lines illustrate the choice that he both contemplated and then took. He wrote:

> Two roads diverged in a yellow wood,
> And sorry I could not travel both…
> I shall be telling this with a sigh
> Somewhere ages and ages hence:
> Two roads diverged in a wood, and I -
> I took the one less traveled by,
> And that has made all the difference.

The book cover depicts the several curves one can encounter in life. No one can go on their life-journey by traveling on a straight path from start to finish. A normal life does not afford one that opportunity. There will be the unexpected and unplanned events that occur, usually subtly and unexpectedly. I posted on Facebook (June 11, 2020) the following: "Cancer is a hideous disease that is no respecter of persons. I have acquaintances and family members who have experienced peaks and valleys as a result of cancer. Psalm 23:4 (NLT) states a truism: "Even when I walk through the darkest valley, I will not be afraid, for you are close beside me." The choice of a key word is "when" rather than "if".

James Perry

There is a certainty that all will come to a place in life when walking through the darkest valley will be a reality.

What are some of the possibilities when one reaches that point in the darkest valley? Personally, we had a son-in-law (Rock) who died at age 30 as a result of cancer; my Great Grandson (Keaton) died at age 8 from Leukemia; and I have had to deal with Lymphoma twice in the past 3 1/2 years. It is easy to understand how Horatio Spafford felt when he reflected on the death of his children in a shipwreck - "When sorrows like sea-billows roll..." There can and will be times, despite one's faith and confidence in Christ alone, when one can feel alone, confused, uncertain and struggling from a sense of being no longer needed or wanted. I know as I have wrestled with this very range of feelings and emotions. The Lord brought to my mind the words of a hymn that expresses the general picture of being overwhelmed by events.

> Just when I am disheartened,
> Just when with cares oppressed,
> Just when my way is darkest,
> Just when I am distressed—
> Then is my Savior near me,
> He knows my every care;
> Jesus will never leave me,
> He helps my burdens bear.

Refrain
> ...His grace is enough for me;
> Through sorrow and pain,

1. The Path We Take

Through loss or gain,
His grace is enough for me.

Just when my hopes are vanished,
Just when my friends forsake,
Just when the fight is thickest,
Just when with fear I shake—
Then comes a still small whisper:
Fear not, My child, I'm near.
Jesus brings peace and comfort,
I love His voice to hear.

Just when my tears are flowing,
when with anguish bent,
Just when temptation's hardest,
Just when with sadness rent—
Then comes a thought of comfort:
I know my Father knows.
Jesus has grace sufficient
To conquer all my foes.

The words underscore for one that which should always be remembered: "Without faith it is IMPOSSIBLE To Please God..." (Hebrews 11:6). In the NIV translation, faith is used 270 times; the derivative faithful is used 83 times; faithfully is used 18 times and faithfulness 59 times. The thrust is that one should never refrain from trusting in the Lord and believing Him for all things. James 1:6-8 (NIV) reminds one: "But when you ask, you must believe and not doubt, because the one who doubts is like a wave of the sea, blown and tossed by the wind. That person should not expect to receive anything from the Lord. Such a person is double-minded and unstable in all they do."

In The Pastor's Blog (June 10, 2020), Charles Swindoll references Ecclesiastes 12:9-11, "Keep this in mind: The Teacher was considered wise, and he taught the people everything he knew. He listened carefully to many proverbs, studying and classifying them. The Teacher sought to find just the right words to express truths clearly. The words of the wise are like cattle prods - painful but helpful..."

He then adds the following application for those called to preach the Word of God. How and when they study for and prepare the sermon is vital – important. He states very pointedly: "Saturday night panic doesn't yield quality stuff on Sunday. A mist in the pulpit puts fog in the pew..."

For the one called by God to preach His Word and to live a life that is an example of what Jesus taught His disciples one must be driven to a basic and simple truth:

> The Lord knows the way through the wilderness,
> All I have to do is follow,,,
> Strength for today, Is mine always –
> And all I need for tomorrow.

1. The Path We Take

The LORD knows the way that I take! Psalm 1:6 (NKJV): "For the LORD knows the way of the righteous, But the way of the ungodly shall perish."

2. Disheartened

Can a servant of the Lord find himself in the arena of despondency, disillusionment, and being disheartened? Yes!

In Chapter One, I reproduced the words from a Hymn where at times the first stanza could be a reality:

> "Just when I am disheartened,
> Just when with cares oppressed,
> Just when my way is darkest,
> Just when I am distressed…"

Why do these emotions fester within one? When I was a young man, a statement made by some preachers was: "I'd rather burn out for the Lord than to rust out for the devil." That phrase stuck with me and mentally is what I wanted – To preach the Word of God rather than sitting idly by while others fulfilled that task. It's part of the mentality of burning out for the Lord rather than rusting out for the devil.

In my first experience with Lymphoma, the PET Scan indicated the Lymph Nodes throughout my body were impacted. The cancer was so great that one Sunday I could not finish preaching a sermon based on Colossians 4:12, "Epaphras prays for you that you might stand firm and fully assured in all the will of God." My second experience with Lymphoma was sudden and a surprise. I was preaching a sermon based upon Romans 12:6-8 (NLT) and one's appreciation for one another's spiritual gifts.

In his grace, God has given us different gifts for doing certain things well. So if God has given you the ability to prophesy, speak out with as much faith as God has given you. If your gift is serving others, serve them well. If you are a teacher, teach well. If your gift is to encourage others, be encouraging. If it is giving, give generously. If God has given you leadership ability, take the responsibility seriously. And if you have a gift for showing kindness to others, do it gladly.

During that Lord's Day it was obvious that I was losing clarity with my voice. My speech was becoming garbled and I was having difficulty swallowing and breathing. On Monday the doctor's examination indicated the lymph nodes in my throat had become enlarged. After several Chemo treatments, the right lymph node was getting larger. The treatment shifted from Chemo to ten days of Radiation. After treatment the lymph nodes are greatly reduced in size and the most recent Pet Scan indicated there is no cancer present.

There are several who have sent words of encouragement to me and my wife and have lifted us up to the throne of grace and mercy during these disheartening times. We are grateful for the several who have become a type of Barnabas to us. We are also grateful for those who have helped us financially. We have used these gifts as they were intended to meet the added costs of travel and treatment for the Lymphoma.

Prior to my second bout with Lymphoma, my Barnabas friend, Steve, had to return for treatment when his Oncologist

2. Disheartened

found a lump that was suspicious. Even with his diagnosis, Steve was still my faithful Barnabas. An early note from my friend whose treatments were challenging and painful included:

> Brother James, there is no doubt that the Lord is not finished with you. You are a gifted writer and bible teacher. Each book I have read from you, especially the last one about Joshua and Caleb's story was a blessing. I understand how you feel, and more importantly so does our Master. One thing is for sure - He is going to take this desert time of suffering to reveal himself greatly in your life and in the lives of those around you…Praying for you mighty man of God, you have been used by the Lord and He isn't finished with you. Love you brother."

Repeatedly, most of the notes received from my special Barnabas begin with: "Praying for you Brother James." Some include: "Praying Psalm 91 for you, Brother James." Psalm 91:1-2 (NIV) states:

> Whoever dwells in the shelter of the Most High will rest in the shadow of the Almighty. I will say of the LORD: He is my refuge and my fortress, my God, in whom I trust.

While I was being both scanned and when receiving Radiation, I tried to recall all of the Scripture I had memorized over the years. I had memorized Psalm 91 as a young boy and it came to me during that time. It kept my mind on the Lord who has promised never to leave or forsake me.

On March 30, 2020, my special Barnabas sent a note:

> How are you making it Brother James. Praying for your healing. Praying that on the tough days of treatment and tough days after treatment that you will feel the embrace of His Grace. May the Lord lift you up on eagle wings.

What is so remarkable about his note is that he had begun a much more severe treatment. A note I received from him in June stated:

> Tomorrow, June 5, will mark one year ago that I entered UAB for my stem cell transplant. I praise the Lord for allowing me to go through this to mature in my faith, to reach the lost and bring Him glory! Thank you for being a man of valor for me. Your prayers and encouragement mean a lot. I am praying for you and your family. Your Servant in Christ, Steve (Psalm 91).

As quickly as I could, I responded:

2. Disheartened

PTL. You have impact in the lives of countless numbers of people - some you may never meet or know until that day when we rejoice together in the presence of Jesus Christ."

In my most downcast moments, I visualized Ethel Waters singing at a Billy Graham Rally in New York City:

> Why should I feel discouraged,
> Why should the shadows come,
> Why should my heart be lonely…
>
> Let not your heart be troubled,
> His tender word I hear,
> And resting on His goodness,
> I lose my doubts and fears…
>
> Though by the path He leadeth,
> But one step I may see…
>
> Whenever I am tempted,
> Whenever clouds arise,
> When songs give place to sighing,
> When hope within me dies…

What is the response to those feelings and emotions? How should one respond to the uncertainties and disappointments in life? The refrain gives an acceptable response:

James Perry

I sing because I'm happy,
I sing because I'm free,
For His eye is on the sparrow,
And I know He watches me.

3. Observation

The Gospel of John has a unique feature. Jesus demonstrates not only who He is, but also what His followers are to learn to be and to do. An early textbook by Merrill C. Tenney (1948) was entitled "The Gospel of Belief." It emphasized the object lessons Jesus was giving not only to the observing multitudes but also to His disciples who would assume ministerial responsibilities in the near future. Tenney's unique emphases includes: Chapter 2 – The first miracle of turning water into wine was one of quality: Chapter 6 – the miracle of turning a young lad's lunch of five loaves and two fish, into food sufficient for more than five-thousand people was one of quantity.

There are other passages that illustrate Jesus's mentoring of - His disciples. In John 13, at the outset of a Passover meal, Jesus washes His disciples feet. He asks them whether or not they have any idea of what He has just done. Rather than allowing or opinion sharing, Jesus states directly that which He has done: "Do you understand what I was doing? You call me Teacher and Lord, and you are right, because that's what I am. And since I, your Lord and Teacher, have washed your feet, you ought to wash each other's feet. I have given you an example to follow. Do as I have done to you." John 13:12-15 (NLT) Jesus is clear. He has given them an example to follow. His directive is: "Do as I have done to you," Be humble and willing to do the menial task. One's body language will speak much more loudly than just one's words.

John 4 records another unique emphases. It will be a learning moment they should embrace and never forget. Jesus was going through Samaria to reach His destination - or – was Samaria the destination? Most Jews would avoid going through Samaria and would avoid the people they despised by taking a much longer route and walking around that area. The text to ponder is John 4:4 (NLT): "He had to go through Samaria on the way." Any translation one consults uses the same idea of "He had to go…" or "He needed to go…"

The text indicates that it was about the noon hour. Jesus had sent His disciples into a nearby town to purchase food. Just as an aside, why did Jesus send all twelve disciples to buy food? What did He have in mind? While they are gone, a woman came to the well to fill her vessel with water. She is a woman with an unsavory and reckless past. Surprisingly, Jesus calls out to her with a request: "Could you get me some water? I am thirsty." At this juncture, the scene shifts dramatically into a discussion and dialogue between the woman and Jesus.

As I've pondered this scene, I have found myself wondering what this even actually was. Was it an interruption in the woman's life? Was he setting the scene up so there would be an intervention as He controlled the dialogue? Would all of this prove to be inconvenient for everyone…anyone? Would there be a time of intercession on behalf of this woman who had lived a wantonly life? Perhaps it was all four – an interruption of her regular routine; an

3. Observation

intervention regarding her lifestyle that she had lived matter-of-factly; an inconvenience since the agenda for the people was now suddenly changed; or a moment when intercession would take place wherein she, and people from her village, would become a new creation in Jesus Christ.

I see it also as a possibility of modelling - The Barnabas Quest (Concept and Principal) for His disciples. Jesus's instruction and miracles were being used as examples of His power at work that would in turn also be available to them. He wanted them to care about the neglected people and those who had been regularly avoided by the religious elite. Jesus wants His disciples to be different. He wants them to have a Barnabas heart. They are to be men who take risks to reach out on behalf of others. They were to set aside any notion of superiority as they learned to walk humbly with their Teacher and Lord.

Can you get a sense of the value and significance of of Jesus Christ in the Samaritan woman's life regardless of her circumstances. What impact does Jesus Christ have on the life and behavior of this woman as a result of this particular ministry? This interaction by Jesus Christ is not dissimilar from what He desires to have with each one of us who are his followers. What can occur by anyone committed enough to desire a Barnabas heart and quest? The disciples will have to know and learn this if they are to effectively serve Jesus Christ. What lesson will the disciples learn as they observe and implement the ensuing response?

James Perry

The lesson Jesus wants his disciples to learn is recounted in John 4:34-35 (NLT): "Jesus explained: My nourishment comes from doing the will of God, who sent me, and from finishing His work. You know the saying: Four months between planting and harvest. But I say, wake up and look around. The fields are already ripe for harvest." When the disciples look around, what do they see? The result of the interaction with the woman at the well is that she had rushed back home and is bringing brought all of the people she could persuade to come and meet a man that had spoken like a prophet to her. John 4:28-30 (NLT) records:

> The woman left her water jar beside the well and ran back to the village, telling everyone: Come and see a man who told me everything I ever did! Could he possibly be the Messiah? So the people came streaming from the village to see him.

Another lesson the disciples will observe and be expected to implement is that Jesus wasn't done with His ministry in Samaria. The people from town begin to urge Jesus to stay and speak further with them. John 4:39-42 (NLT) records:

> Many Samaritans from the village believed in Jesus because the woman had said: He told me everything I ever did! When they came out to see him, they begged him to stay in their village. So he stayed for two days, long enough for many more to hear his message and

3. Observation

believe. Then they said to the woman: Now we believe, not just because of what you told us, but because we have heard Him ourselves. Now we know that He is indeed the Savior of the world.

What a dramatic turn of events. Most "believers" would've bypassed Sychar in Samaria and taken a longer journey to avoid having to see or talk with the Samaritans. The Samaritans don't like the Jews. The Jews viewed the Samaritans as "dogs" with whom they refused any association. The disciples had a lesson to learn from these events in Sychar. When one is serving Jesus Christ, traditions, ethnic distinctions, racial differences, current events all pale when compared with the mission Jesus has in mind to pierce through the darkness so that the lost may see the light and come to Him.

> Far, far away, in heathen darkness dwelling,
> Millions of souls forever may be lost;
> Who, who will go, salvation's story-telling,
> Looking to Jesus, heeding not the cost?

Refrain:
> All power is given unto Me...

> Go ye into all the world and preach the Gospel,
> And lo, I am with you always.

> See o'er the world wide open doors inviting,

James Perry

Soldiers of Christ, arise and enter in!
Christians, awake! your forces all uniting,
Send forth the Gospel, break the chains of sin.

4. Intercession

As the disciples observed the ministry of Jesus Christ with the Samaritan woman, what major lesson should they have seen? What lesson must they learn from Him? At the very least, His interaction led to the moment of intercession on an unpredictable scale. Jesus not only addresses the religious and traditional misconceptions of the woman, but an extended intercession with the people from her home village. Interestingly, there were no other character names mentioned in this divine moment. The reference is to a needy woman and then her fellow-villagers.

Jesus shared an important insight on intercession. In John 17:6-19 (NLT), contains The High Priestly Prayer of Jesus Christ. Jesus had come to a point where He was concluding His training of His disciples and was preparing for the moment for which He had come. His prayer includes:

> I have revealed you to the ones you gave me from this world. They were always yours. You gave them to me, and they have kept your word. Now they know that everything I have is a gift from you, for I have passed on to them the message you gave me. They accepted it and know that I came from you, and they believe you sent me. My prayer is not for the world, but for those you have given me, because they belong

to you. All who are mine belong to you, and you have given them to me, so they bring me glory....

Make them (the disciples) holy by your truth; teach them your word, which is truth. Just as you sent me into the world, I am sending them into the world...

I am praying not only for these disciples but also for all who will believe in me through their message.

What role does Jesus Christ have in the lives of those who believe in Him today? The disciples had the unique privilege of personally observing, hearing, learning and believing Jesus. They were aware of His prayer of intercession on their behalf. They were also aware of His praying for those who would hear the message of the Lord from the disciples and then believe. It is refreshing to read and know the words spoken about Jesus, the great high priest who offered Himself once for all as the sacrifice for one's sin: He (Jesus Christ) is able to save to the uttermost those who draw near to God through him, since He always lives to make intercession for them" Hebrews 7:25 (ESV). One should greatly appreciate this continuing ministry of Jesus Christ that is defined as: "He always lives to make intercession for them (us)."

Intercession includes the activity of the Holy Spirit on behalf of those who have believed and are following Jesus Christ. When the disciples asked Jesus how to pray, Jesus gave them a prayer – The Lord's Prayer (Matthew 6 and Luke 11) – as a model. Some mistakenly believe that if they quote the model prayer their needs will be met by The Lord.

4. Intercession

However, just a brief outline of the prayer should grant one an insight that The Lord's Prayer is a guideline one should follow rather using the precise words as a potential "vain repetition." The Prayer leads one to:

(1) Worship Our Father
  (a) Who resides in Heaven
  (b) His name is to be hallowed
  (c) His Kingdom is to be sought
  (d) His will is to be known and done
(2) Express personal needs
  (a) Provisional needs such as daily food
  (b) Forgiving one's sins even as they one forgives the sins of others
  (c) Guard one against temptation and the prevailing evil that is in the world
(3) End with a Benediction at the conclusion of the model prayer
  (a) Yours is the Kingdom
  (b) Yours is the Power
  (c) Yours is the Glory - forever

How is intercession understood and activated in behalf of the people of God today? We gain an important insight in Romans 8:26-27 (ESV):

> Likewise the Spirit helps us in our weakness. For we do not know what to pray for as we ought, but the

Spirit himself intercedes for us with groanings too deep for words. And he who searches hearts knows what is the mind of the Spirit, because the Spirit intercedes for the saints according to the will of God."

When this ministry is understood, it allows one to confidently know and claim Romans 8:28 (ESV) as a component of one's faith and practice: "We know that for those who love God all things work together for good, for those who are called according to his purpose."

Who are those who are called according to His purpose? Romans 8:29-30 (ESV) clarifies:

> "For those whom He foreknew He also predestined to be conformed to the image of his Son…And those whom he predestined he also called, and those whom he called he also justified, and those whom he justified he also glorified."

If you are called according to the purpose of God for your life, then you should be assured that the Holy Spirit is interceding for you so that your prayer(s) conform to the will of God for your life.

> I belong to the King, and He loves me I know,
> For His mercy and kindness so free
> Are unceasingly mine wheresoever I go,
> And my refuge unfailing is He.

4. Intercession

Refrain:
    I belong to the King; I'm a child of His love,
    And he never forsaketh His own.
    He will call me some day to His palace above;
    I shall dwell by His glorified throne.

5. Availability

When my wife and I discussed our future together, one of the points of agreement was our willingness to go anywhere, at any time, to do any work, at any cost. We thought we might be going in the direction of a mission field. We were inclined to apply to the China Inland Mission so we could minister to the Chinese people. In the late 40s and early 50s, the political orientation of China was transitioning into communism and the missionaries were no longer welcomed to live and share the Gospel message there. As that door shut we came to the conclusion that we should pursue pastoral ministry and set out to do so.

Along the way, we met some people who became special friends. Some were gifted at doing the Barnabas style ministry with others and we benefitted from that encouragement and prayerful support. My belief is that it is essential to know those who are similar to Barnabas and are willing to take risks on the behalf of others.

If we are generous in our Biblical exegesis, we will find the Barnabas type individuals at different intervals in Biblical History. A brief scan indicates that Moses had Joshua (as well as Aaron and Miriam); Joshua had Caleb (a relationship that exceeded more than forty-five years); David had Jonathan; Hezekiah had Isaiah; Daniel had his three friends. The list could be much longer as one thinks through Scripture and the significant difference that was made by those who invested their lives and ministry in that of another.

When I was first diagnosed with stage four Lymphoma in 2017, a man, Steve Sellers, whom I had never known or met made contact with me via a personal note on Facebook. He was employed by the Alabama Baptist Children's Home to visit the churches and raise support for the ministry for children with varying needs. He shared with me that he had received the same stage four Lymphoma diagnoses earlier and was now in his fifth year of remission. It was a great encouragement for me as I wondered about and pondered what was occurring in my body and life. At that point, I was thinking about the worst scenario and my need to get matters in order so my wife and family would be able to conduct the household affairs without any hindrances.

My friendship with Steve has continued and we have shared personal matters with each other. The Lord uses a wide range of individuals to fulfill a Barnabas ministry in the life of another. One incident shared by Steve is about a little boy who had nothing but became a Barnabas to Steve at an appropriate time when the boy's intercession was needed most. On December 23, 2018, Steve shared the following:

This broken Christmas cookie is over 15 years old. It has been in my freezer for that long. To you it may appear as just another Christmas cookie, but it is one of the greatest acts of encouragement and reminder of God's call upon my life.

5. Availability

My role at Alabama Baptist Children's Homes is to raise funds and to encourage churches to partner with ABCH. My father-in-law when he was alive called me a beggar. That's okay because I will plead the cause of the fatherless and invite folks to make a gift that has an impact on lives for eternity

There are days when I am well received when visiting and then there are days that are tough. Such was the day that I received a gift of encouragement, a hug from my Heavenly Father.

I had visited with a business owner to see about a gift. The owner's response: It is not my responsibility to care for these kids, it's the government's. I left the business with a grieved spirit, because of this person's attitude.

My next visit with a pastor did not go so well either. I shared about the Annual Offering and how the special offering helps ABCH to minister to those in our care. The answer was basically: You are not a part of our mission focus. I certainly understand from being a pastor that they and the church are asked to support a lot of mission efforts. The words of John Steward ring in my heart: Tell Baptists what you need and they will do the rest.

After that meeting I thought to myself: I'm not so sure. I know that Alabama Baptists are second milers that they not only give through the Cooperative Program, but they have many churches who give through their budgets or special offering. Just giving a picture of what that day was like.

The day was rejection after rejection, so that by the late afternoon discouragement had covered my heart. I thought it is just time to quit, go do something else. Have you ever been there friend?

The Holy Spirit in a still small voice said: You need to go by the group home. Lord, I will go, but I am still quitting!

I met a little boy who had not been there long, he said: Hi mister and he introduced himself. I will not share his real name, but I will just call him Jimmy. Jimmy had a smile that would capture anyone's heart. He had come from a hard place to this place of refuge. You would think that a little boy who had been so wounded would never be able to smile again, but the embrace of Grace has a way of changing children and adults.

I got ready to leave when I felt a tug on my pants leg. I looked down into the smiling face of Jimmy. He had this Christmas cookie. Some Women's Missionary Union ladies in the area had made Cookies for the kids to enjoy at Christmas time. I knelt down and asked: What can I do for you Jimmy? With that beautiful smile he responded: Merry Christmas Mr. Steve. I was speechless over this tremendous gift from a child. The house parent informed me that was Jimmy's last Christmas cookie of the gift the ladies had provided to each child. I hugged him and responded: Merry Christmas Jimmy.

When I left, I only drove about a mile until I had to pull over. I sat in a church parking lot holding this most valuable gift and wept. Then the Lord spoke to my heart: Son, you are doing this work for me and for kids. My Heavenly Father had met me that day and through the gift of a Christmas Cookie encouraged me to Keep On Keeping On.

5. Availability

There are still days of discouragement. Days of where I feel I have failed. Days of deadlines and miles to travel. Days of wondering how this need will be met. When those days come I look at this Christmas Cookie to remind me how my Lord encouraged me through a little boy name Jimmy. The King reminds this servant of my Mission Assignment and that He is the Provider. The cookie over time is broken from handling and being old, but it still used by the Lord to Encourage me. So you see it's not just another Christmas Cookie. It was a telegram of Love and Encouragement from the Lord through His (Barnabas) messenger Jimmy.

So, friend, if you feel like quitting this Christmas don't. The same God who blessed me through this Christmas Cookie wants to do the same for you. Just crawl up into His lap this morning and feel the warmth of His Embrace of Grace.

It brings to mind the Hymn written in 1877 by Mary M. Dodge who wrote the song for the younger children. As she noted: "For very Little Folks."

>Can a little child like me
>Thank the Father fittingly?
>Yes, oh yes! be good and true,
>Faithful, kind, in all you do;
>Love the Lord, and do your part;
>Learn to say with all your heart,
>Father, we thank Thee,
>Father, we thank Thee,
>Father in Heaven, we thank Thee

6. Readiness

In the process of the training of the twelve, there came a special moment when the disciples made a request of their Teacher. Luke 11:1 (NIV) makes known their request: "One day Jesus was praying in a certain place. When he finished, one of his disciples said to him: Lord, teach us to pray, just as John taught his disciples." No mention is made of which disciple came to Jesus representing the others and said: "Teach us to pray." The words of an older hymn reflect the same sentiment:

> Teach me to pray, Lord, teach me to pray;
> This is my heart-cry day unto day;
> I long to know Thy will and Thy way;
> Teach me to pray, Lord, teach me to pray.

Refrain:
> Living in Thee, Lord, and Thou in me,
> Constant abiding, this is my plea;
> Grant me Thy power, boundless and free,
> Power with men and power with Thee.

> Power in prayer, Lord, power in prayer!
> Here 'mid earth's sin and sorrow and care,
> Men lost and dying, souls in despair;
> O give me power, power in prayer!

It reminded me of some phrases in another older Hymn, Once To Every Man and Nation. The first stanza includes:

> Once to every man and nation,
> Comes the moment to decide,
> In the strife of truth with falsehood,
> For the good or evil side;
> Some great cause, some great decision...

The disciples made a wise decision when they asked Jesus to teach them to pray just as John the Baptist had taught his disciples. Rather than duplicate the prayers taught by John the Baptist, the Lord responds to that serious and sincere request by sharing a prayer guideline with them as to what they should set as a priority when they pray (Luke 11:1-4; Matthew 6:9-13).The guideline is divided into three primary areas: (1) begin with Worship and Acknowledgement of the Eternal God and Creator who resides in heaven; (2) make practical requests based upon need rather than greed; and (3) seek forgiveness for personal debts and those who are indebted to them, along with the spirit and attitude that seeks personal forgiveness for one's sins and trespasses, as well of forgiving the sins and trespasses of others.

Jesus is very precise and careful to underscore that which their prayer must include. Jesus with "Thy kingdom come" so that the disciples...and we....would know His stated order of

6. Readiness

petitions. The order of petitions is actually intercessory in character and form. The forgiveness of others, which is the measure and plea of our own forgiveness, brings even those who have wronged us upon the same plane as ourselves. And if the plea be genuine, how can we refuse to pray for them? And if one prays for ones enemies, then surely there should be attention given to pray equally for one's friends. The utilization of intercessory prayer cannot be neglected or absent as one prays.

The spirit of intercession is found in the pleas of those who sought Christ's help for their friends. Examples include:

(1) Matthew 8:13 - the centurion and his concern for his servant

(2) Matthew 9:2-6 – The friends coming by faith to Jesus and seeking help and relief for their paralytic friend

(3) Matthew 15:28 – the persistent request of a mother for her child and the Lord's response

(4) Matthew 17:14-21 – the man with a lunatic son asking for help and healing

Matthew 20:20-23 is an illustration of an unexpected, inappropriate intercession when the mother of Zebedee's sons (James and John) makes a request on behalf of her children for a place of honor and authority for them in the kingdom of Jesus Christ. If only the mother had interceded that her sons might possess a heart and conscience of compassion wherein they could develop the character to enable them to function as a comforter and encourager. In a troubled culture and world, there is an increasing need for those who will stand in the gap and resist the trend away from God and His Word.

Francis Schaeffer did much of his writing in the 1960s and 1970s. In his book, *Death In The City*, he wrote:

> We live in a post-Christian world. What should be our perspective as individuals, as institutions, as orthodox Christians, as those who claim to be Bible-believing? How should we look at this post-Christian world and function as Christians in it?
>
> Ours is a post-Christian world in which Christianity, not only in the number of Christians but in cultural emphasis and cultural result, is now in the minority.
>
> The Bible puts its religious teaching in a historic setting. It is quite the opposite of the new theology and existential thought...Our generation takes the word religion and everything religious and turns it into something psychological or sociological.
>
> A holy and a loving God really exists, and He works into the significant history which exists. He works in history on the basis of His character; and when His people and their culture turn away from Him, He works in history in judgment.
>
> Man is not just a chance configuration of atoms in the slipstream of meaningless chance history. Man, made in the image of God, has a purpose - to be in

6. Readiness

relationship to the God who is there. Whether it is in Jeremiah's day, or in our own recent generations, the effect is the same. Man forgets his purpose, and thus he forgets who he is and what life means.

Today we are left largely not only with a religion and a church without meaning, but we are left with a culture without meaning. Man himself is dead.

What marks our own generation? It is the fact that modern man thinks there is nobody home in the universe. Nobody to love man, nobody to comfort him, even while he seeks desperately to find comfort in the limited, finite, horizontal relationships of life.

Without saying it directly he is indicating that there is a need of a Jeremiah who will weep over Jerusalem and a people who have turned their backs to the Lord. There is a great need for disciples of intercession to step forward and be known as well as heard. There is a great vacuum that longs for The Barnabas Quest to accelerate. There is a need for many people in all walks of life and age groups to become those who will step into the gap with credibility, integrity, courage and compassion.

A Hymn expresses well how one should model readiness to be whatever the Lord wants him/her to be and do. The time is short and the need is immediate. The Hymn includes:

> So send I you to labor unrewarded,
> To serve unpaid, unloved, unsought, unknown,

James Perry

To bear rebuke, to suffer scorn and scoffing...

So send I you to bind the bruised and broken,
Over wandering souls to work, to weep, to wake,
To bear the burdens of a world a-weary...

So send I you to loneliness and longing...

So send I you to leave your life's ambition,
To die to dear desire, self-will resign...

Are you equal to such a calling and task? Do you believe God's grace will be more than sufficient for you as you become a Barnabas-type servant for Him? Trust Him – He will be more than enough for all He calls you to do for Him.

7. Willingness

The Barnabas Quest is not the easiest pathway for one to travel. An inner struggle can take place. The tension arises between readiness on the one hand and reluctance on the other. We have all become too comfortable with an old saying – "the spirit is willing but the flesh is weak." We may not all have said it aloud but inwardly most of us know that inner struggle. Should I go or stay? Should I volunteer or excuse myself from any responsibility? Should I be affirmative or negative? Should I encourage the subject and request or deny and discourage it?

There is an humorous old story about willingness and how one or another responds to taking responsibilities and fulfilling them. It tells of people all of whom have reasons for being busy and find it easy to pass an opportunity on to someone else rather than taking on the responsibility for themselves. It demonstrates why team work, personal interest, communication and leadership are important in doing any work.

> The story is about four people whose names are Everybody, Somebody, Anybody, and Nobody. There was an important job to be done and Everybody was sure that Somebody would do it. Anybody could have done it, but Nobody did it. Somebody got angry about that because it was Everybody's job. Everybody

thought that Anybody could do it but Nobody realized that Everybody wouldn't do it. It ended up that Everybody blamed Somebody when Nobody did what Anybody could have done.

There are some interesting Biblical situations when the Lord issues a call for a person to serve Him in a particular way and the person called isn't so willing to take on the responsibility. One such instance was God's call to Moses to lead His people out of bondage. Rather than immediately responding enthusiastically and willingly, Moses offered a series of excuses (Exodus 3 and 4). The issue crystalized and the Lord's anger became evident. If it was possible for the Lord to become exasperated, Moses had driven Him to that point.

Inasmuch as Moses kept making excuses as to why he was unfit and incapable of doing that which the Lord was calling Him and promising to equip him to do, the Lord listened and then responded to Moses in Exodus 4:13-16 (NIV),

> But Moses said: Pardon your servant, Lord. Please send someone else. Then the LORD's anger burned against Moses and he said: What about your brother, Aaron the Levite? I know he can speak well. He is already on his way to meet you, and he will be glad to see you. You shall speak to him and put words in his mouth; I will help both of you speak and will teach you what to do. He will speak to the people for you, and it

7. Willingness

will be as if he were your mouth and as if you were God to him.

Other illustrations could be shared about those who were hesitant or reluctant to accept the task the Lord wanted them to do. There is the situation with Gideon when the Lord calls him to fight the Midianites (see: Judges 6:13-16). There is a similar Moses-type moment when the Lord is calling Jeremiah to be his prophet (see: Jeremiah 1:4-10).

There is a refreshing response from Isaiah when the Lord reveals Himself from His heaven (Isaiah 6 and presents the near-impossible task of reaching a rebellious people. The Lord poses a question and Isaiah responds (Isaiah 6:7-9), "Then I heard the voice of the Lord saying: Whom shall I send? And who will go for us? And I said: Here am I. Send me! And the Lord said: Go and tell this people..." The message to be delivered would be one of confrontation and the pending judgment of the Lord. Regardless of the best effort put forward by Isaiah, The Lord indicates that the people will not hear the message nor will they respond affirmatively to correct anything about their lifestyle choices. Isaiah never offers an excuse. Having seen the Lord in His holiness, Isaiah responds willingly and responsibly.

There is another refreshing moment in the ministry of the Lord Jesus Christ. Following His temptation by the devil in the wilderness and His victory over him, Jesus begins to prepare for His brief earthly ministry. This includes His calling disciples who will join and follow Him. One place where this is chronicled is Matthew 4:17-22.

> As Jesus was walking beside the Sea of Galilee, he saw two brothers, Simon called Peter and his brother Andrew. They were casting a net into the lake, for they were fishermen. Come, follow me, Jesus said, and I will send you out to fish for people. At once they left their nets and followed him. Going on from there, he saw two other brothers, James son of Zebedee and his brother John. They were in a boat with their father Zebedee, preparing their nets. Jesus called them, and immediately they left the boat and their father and followed him.

Peter, Andrew, James or John didn't ask any questions or make any excuses. It is stated that Peter and Andrew "at once" left their nets to follow Jesus; with James and John the term used is "immediately" they left their boat and father's business to follow Jesus Christ. Did these four men know what they being called to be and do? No! Did they desire to know why they were the ones called instead of those who were better qualified? No! Did they know how long they would have to be with Jesus and follow Him? No! There was no hesitancy or reluctance on their part – only willingness, eagerness and forsaking all to follow Jesus.

7. Willingness

In The Barnabas Quest, how does Jesus want His people to respond to Him as and when He calls? A response is found in the words of a hymn:

>Hast Thou, O Lord, a work to do?
>Here am I, send me!
>The field is white, the laborers few,
>Here am I, send me!
>Refrain:
>Over mountain, plain or sea,
>Here am I, send me!
>I'll go to the ends of the earth for Thee,
>Here am I, send me!
>
>My heart now longs and yearns to go,
>Here am I, send me!
>To reap Thy harvest here below,
>Here am I, send me!

8. Teachability

When Jesus called men to follow Him and to learn from Him, He set no time frame for their training. His training method was different inasmuch as it did not follow any established rabbinical methodology nor would it follow an established Seminary-type curriculum. The training He had in mind was a lifetime of learning, understanding, applying and doing. This is why He stated (Luke 9:23 – NIV), "He said to them all: Whoever wants to be my disciple must deny themselves and take up their cross daily and follow me." It is worded differently (personalized) in the NLT, "Then he said to the crowd: If any of you wants to be My follower, you must give up your own way, take up your cross daily, and follow Me." The MSG wording is: "Then he told them what they could expect for themselves: Anyone who intends to come with Me has to let Me lead. You're not in the driver's seat—I am. Don't run from suffering; embrace it. Follow Me and I'll show you how. Self-help is no help at all. Self-sacrifice is the way, My way, to finding yourself, your true self."

It reminded me of some words contained in a Hymn written by Fanny Crosby about discipleship commitment:

> If My disciple thou wouldst be,
> Take up the cross and follow Me…

> Bearing the cross in good or ill,
> Trusting the hand that guides thee still…

James Perry

There is a crown of life for thee;
Take up the cross and follow Me.

In a portion of a June 14, 2020 devotional by Charles Swindoll he writes about the place and need for suffering:

> Suffering: Down through the centuries it has been God's taming ground for raging bulls. The crucible of pain and hardship is God's schoolroom where Christians learn humility, compassion, character, patience, and grace. It's true for you and for me...I don't understand all the reasons we suffer for the Name. But I'm convinced of this: it is part of God's sovereign plan to prepare us to be His instruments of grace to a harsh and desperate world. Clearly, this is often God's plan...

Daily discipleship training may result in several unexpected experiences and human surprises. The person I have referred to as "my Barnabas" (Steve Sellers) has proven to be a faithful encourager in my life. Although we have never met personally nor spoken with each other, we have corresponded regularly with one another over the past three years or so. We were both rejoicing in the cancer remission status the Lord had blest us with – when suddenly, I received a note from Steve early in 2019 that his Oncologist was concerned about a lump (node) that he believed needed to be checked out. It would require Steve to spend time in the

8. Teachability

Hospital and be subjected to painful medical procedures. He always endured it positively. At that point, I believed that I could reverse the Barnabas role and reciprocate with Steve by being an encourager for and with him.

That role reversal did not last very long. In the latter part of February 2020, I realized that something was happening with my throat. My speech was slowly becoming slurred, I was gagging frequently when trying to swallow anything, and I was laboring in my breathing. The Ear, Nose and Throat Specialist confirmed that I had a growth in my throat that did not belong there. He ordered a PET Scan and determined that it appeared to be an infected lymph-node. I was sent to the Manderson Cancer Center in Tuscaloosa, AL and aggressive Chemotherapy began. Following the fourth Chemo treatment, the growth on the right side had enlarged. I was sent to a Radiation Oncologist and radiation treatments began for the better part of two weeks.

I was trying to continue to be a Barnabas for Steve even amid my growing concern for my own situation. I rejoiced when word from Steve was received that indicated: "June 5, 2020 will mark one year ago that I entered UAB (University of Alabama Medical Center in Birmingham, AL) for my Stem Cell Implant. Praise the Lord for allowing me to go through this to mature me in my faith to enable me to reach the lost, and to bring Him glory."

Then, my Barnabas wrote to me (who was attempting to be his Barnabas): "Thank you for being a man of valor for me.

Your prayers and encouragement mean a lot. I am praying for you. Your Servant in Christ – Steve (Psalm 91)."

Do we – can we – always understand what God is doing in our lives? No! Can we easily accept why He is doing the unexpected (and unwanted)? No! Does God unpredictably provide a word of encouragement in His perfect timing? Yes!

As I was pondering these and other thoughts, a bookmark from Charles Stanley (June 13, 2020) suddenly surfaced on my desk (after a stack of papers and cards piled on my desk had slipped over) that shared this thought: "Psalm 81 - In difficult times, you won't understand everything God is doing. Trust He is in control, and stay close to Him in prayer and praise. He will carry you through." Perfect timing by the perfect Lord and Master.

Perhaps you remember from years ago when the combination of letters BPWMGIDWMY circulated and aroused curiosity. What do these letters represent and mean? It is a truth that no disciple in a life-time and daily training should ever forget: BPWMGIDWMY – Be Patient With Me God Isn't Done With Me Yet. It reminded me also of a cute poster one of our children posted alongside of her bed. It was a lovely picture and the caption was: "God Doesn't Make No Junk!"

The Lord continues His daily process of training each one to be a more efficient as a disciple for Him. It is also the process that includes one being conformed more and more to His image. Be reminded of God's objective for you – First

8. Teachability

Peter 1:12-14 (NLT)

Prepare your minds for action and exercise self-control. Put all your hope in the gracious salvation that will come to you when Jesus Christ is revealed to the world. So you must live as God's obedient children. Don't slip back into your old ways of living to satisfy your own desires. You must be holy in everything you do, just as God who chose you is holy.

9. Scriptualization

During my pre-teen years, I had a Sunday School teacher who insisted that the boys in his class memorize Scripture. The first text he assigned was Proverbs 4:23 (KJV), "Keep thy heart with all diligence; for out of it are the issues of life." The NLT is: "Guard your heart above all else, for it determines the course of your life." The teacher's strategy followed that of the Psalmist who wrote: "I have hidden your word in my heart that I might not sin against you" (Psalm 119:11 - NIV). And: "Your word is a lamp for my feet, a light on my path" (Psalm 119:105 – NIV). In his letter to Timothy, Paul addresses the dangers of the last days and the expanding evil that will prevail (Second Timothy 3:1-8). He also reminds Timothy of the important place of Scripture for the follower of Jesus Christ. In Second Timothy 3:14-17 (NLT), Paul writes Timothy and states:

> But you must remain faithful to the things you have been taught. You know they are true, for you know you can trust those who taught you. You have been taught the holy Scriptures from childhood, and they have given you the wisdom to receive the salvation that comes by trusting in Christ Jesus. All Scripture is inspired by God and is useful to teach us what is true and to make us realize what is wrong in our lives. It corrects us when we are wrong and teaches us to do

what is right. God uses it to prepare and equip his people to do every good work.

When Joshua was chosen to replace Moses and to lead God's people into the Promised Land, the Lord challenged and directed Joshua as to what he was expected to do as the leader of God's people. We learn these words in Joshua 1:8 (NLT), "Study this Book of Instruction continually. Meditate on it day and night so you will be sure to obey everything written in it. Only then will you prosper and succeed in all you do." Knowledge of and obedience to Scripture allowed Joshua to both prosper and succeed in all areas of his work and life.

As I was being scanned and receiving radiation for Lymphoma, rather than focus on the hardness and discomfort of the X-ray table, I recalled most of the Scripture I had memorized, as well as Hymns I had learned and sung over the years. I regularly post some of these verses and hymns on Facebook. My Barnabas, Steve, touched my heart several times as he shared one Scripture in particular with me. When he was downcast and being subjected to a very important treatment, he was emotionally overwhelmed. When a Nurse inquired how he was, he asked her to read a passage of Scripture to him – Psalm 91. This is a passage that has sustained him throughout the years of cancer treatment and ancillary procedures. Interestingly, it was a Psalm that the faithful Sunday School Teacher had his pre-teen boys memorize.

9. Scriptualization

Some of the Verses from Psalm 91 that are reassuring and have special application include:

He who dwells in the shelter of the Most High
will abide in the shadow of the Almighty. I will say to the LORD, He is –
- My refuge and
- My fortress, and
- My God, in whom I trust.

Because you have made the LORD your dwelling place—the Most High, who is my refuge no evil shall be allowed to befall you, no plague come near your tent...

Because he holds fast to me in love, I will deliver him; I will protect him, because he knows my name. When he calls to me,
- I will answer him;
- I will be with him in trouble;
- I will rescue him and honor him.
- With long life I will satisfy him and show him my salvation.

Two other passages of Scripture that guided me through the peaks and valleys of cancer treatment include Psalm 118:4-5, "Let those who fear the LORD say, His loving devotion endures forever. In my distress I called to the LORD, and He answered and set me free." Being set free included added strength and inward peace. When one hears the diagnosis of being Stage 4 Non-Hodgkin Lymphoma, fear is ready to pounce and causes one to think in terms of one's days being numbered. When I returned home after my first treatments in 2018, the medications I was receiving caused to faint. I was walking down the hallway of our home on my way to the Family Room only to regain consciousness and find myself on the hallway floor. My wife called the local police who came and picked me up and suggested I stay in the recliner and avoid a repeat.

As the days progressed, I was feeling alright and felt I was regaining strength. It was a chilly and cold morning and I decided to light a fire in the fireplace. At 4:00 A.M., I decided to go out the side door and get a few sticks of firewood. I was doing fine until I bent over to pick up a fallen stick. Once again, I passed out. This time I was in my pajamas and bedroom shoes. When I fell, it was on the gravel section of our driveway and I was unable to get up. I was getting colder and colder but there was no one driving by at that hour that could stop and assist me. I tried crawling toward the back door but there was a low brick finishing wall that I was unable to get over. I was crawling and trying to get myself upright for almost 40 minutes. What else could I do with thin clothes and bare feet on a cold morning.

I did remember to pray and a verse of Scripture that became very meaningful in that distressful moment was Psalm 34:4, "I sought the LORD, and He answered me; He delivered me from all my fears." Within a few minutes (that seemed more like hours), my wife appeared at the kitchen door and saw my plight. We keep a walker in our home. My wife got it

9. Scriptualization

and with it and her assistance, after much effort and increasing weakness, I was able to get upright and re-enter the warm home.

No one should ever underestimate the benefit of Scripture. It is always applicable and practical. A phrase that occurred to me then and oftentimes afterwards is found in Isaiah 41:10-11, "Do not fear, for I am with you; do not be afraid, for I am your God. I will strengthen you; I will surely help you; I will uphold you with My right hand of righteousness." The brief phrase in Isaiah 43:5 is also reassuring: "Do not be afraid, for I am with you…" The words that are given to Joshua are also very practical, Deuteronomy 31:8, "The LORD himself goes before you and will be with you; He will never leave you nor forsake you. Do not be afraid; do not be discouraged."

One of the side effects that can occur with a cancer patient who is having Chemotherapy is Chemo-Brain. It's as though the mental gears try to avoid meshing. It comes and goes for some, whereas others have been spared such moments. A Hymn that helped me to gain and maintain spiritual focus is:

> Why should I feel discouraged,
> Why should the shadows come,
> Why should my heart be lonely…
> When Jesus is my portion…
> I know He (Jesus) watches me…
>
> Let not your heart be troubled,
> His tender word I hear,

> And resting on His goodness,
> I lose my doubts and fears...
> I know He (Jesus) watches me...

My Barnabas (Steve) has faithfully upheld me in prayer and sent me timely words of encouragement. Several of you who read this chapter have also been faithful in your prayers and at various times when you have encouraged my wife and me. Thank you for caring and praying. Thank you, Steve, for reminding me that God isn't done with me yet!

10. Candidates

Is there a need for a Barnabas-type ministry in the contemporary Church? If it is necessary, who can qualify for serving in this capacity? What is the expectation of a functional Barnabas in today's culture and world? Are there individuals, families or groups that would welcome those filling the role of a Barnabas reaching out to them? Should it be publicly announced or advertised that someone or some organization is available to be an encourager and/or consoler? Can it/Should it be organized as a rehabilitation organization or unit? If it is organized as a rehabilitation group, what will the primary focus be?

By definition, rehabilitation is "a program or facility for treating persons addicted to drugs or alcohol or recovering from certain medical and/or mental conditions." There is an organization called Barnabas Ministries who state their focused Mission, Vision and Statement of Faith:

> Our Mission: Barnabas Ministries is passionately committed to reaching high risk youth and families with the message of freedom, hope, and healing found only in Jesus Christ. Our Vision: To create an environment where hurting youth and families can discover their value in Christ, grow in that knowledge, and pass that knowledge on to others. Our Values: Christ-centered, Biblically Based, Local Church

Connected, Prayer Dependent, Relationally Focused, Volunteer Driven.

They have also published a lengthy Statement of Faith that is general in its form.

There is an old saying that being a disciple of Jesus Christ is more caught than taught. To be a servant of the Lord is more of an individual commitment rather than one made after being screened by a Board of Directors; or a religious group examination; or a psychological panel that decides one has the emotional qualities to perform a ministry task.

What should a Barnabas-type look like today? There is no precise Biblical instruction. It is my persuasion that the numerous "one another/each other" passages throughout the Bible (especially in the New Testament) indicate some of the basic qualities needed by anyone doing a Barnabas ministry. Those who like to tally up different phrases in Scripture have noted there are at least fifty-nine "one another/each other" references in the New Testament.

When I was a youth (pre-teen and teen), I attended a small independent church in Brooklyn, New York. Part of my motivation to attend was because they had a basketball team that played in a league and they gave free musical lessons on instruments they provided so one could participate in their band that performed Salvation Army Marching Band Music. As a church group, they also had a "ritual" on Sundays when The Lord's Supper was presented. Everyone was supposed to know (preferably memorize) and recite two passages of

10. Candidates

Scripture before partaking of the Sacrament – I Corinthians 13 and Romans 12.

Prior to my losing clarity in speech and having to suspend public speaking and preaching in February 2020, I had begun a series of sermons on the "one another" passages. I was preaching the third sermon of the series and was using the text in Romans 12:9-13 with the emphasis of what a minimum vision and practice of ministry by all of God's people should include. The passage could be considered as a preamble to a godly job description for how God's people are to live, act and serve. The text contains the following:

> Be devoted to one another in love.
> Honor one another above yourselves.
> Never be lacking in zeal, but keep your spiritual fervor, serving the Lord.
> Be joyful in hope, patient in affliction, faithful in prayer.
> Share with the Lord's people who are in need.
> Practice hospitality.

How do you measure up to these brief requirements? Is this something you are committed to live by and do in a functional manner? If studied, would the fifty-nine one another and each other passages in the New Testament, describe you as a person and servant of the Lord?

When I was first admitted into the Hospital in 2017 for my initial procedures (Tracheotomy and PEG Feeding Tube), a preliminary interview question was: "Have you thought about suicide or taking your own life in the past two weeks?" Time after time that question was posed prior to receiving the chemotherapy infusion. The question became annoying to me inasmuch as I know that the Lord has determined the precise day and hour when He will welcome me into His heaven and I believe that to be absent from the body is to be present with the Lord. One of the things that bothered me the most about the suicide question was that no Hospital Chaplain came around to visit and discuss spiritual matters. There was only one time that a volunteer Chaplain's Assistant passed by each patient in a large room to determine why they were there and how they were feeling. That was it. Very short and matter-of-fact – and – away she went.

What I like about "My Barnabas" (Steve) is that he is faithful and timely. He has a God-given sense of the right time and moment to write – "Mighty man of God – I'm praying for you." He is regular in his follow-up and I'm convinced that at any time I contacted him, he would stop what he was doing and either pray for me, or if need be, find time to visit with me. I've never broached that situation with him and don't feel that I need to do so. His faithful approach is contagious and I have found myself contacting people who have a need and trying to be a Barnabas to them.

One day in June 2020, I was "thinking out loud" when I wrote an entry on Facebook. It wasn't written to solicit commiserating or testimonials. I was lamenting the fact that I felt ready to return to the pulpit and resume preaching the

10. Candidates

Word once again – BUT – there was no longer any place where I was invited to come and fill the pulpit. It was one of those downcast – feeling sorry for myself – kind of days and moments. When fifty-six years of one's life has been attempting to faithfully preach God's Word and suddenly it appears there is no longer any need to assist the church in that way – the devil took the opportunity and tried to discourage me.

Several positive comments were shared by dear ones - each of them a Barnabas in his or her own way – words of encouragement and gratitude. Just a few thoughts that were shared: "Prayers are being said for you. You are being held up to the Lord to receive His grace and mercy." Another shared: "Know this, You, dear Sir, are Pastor to so many here on Facebook – for those of us worshipping and serving from our homes." Then this word: "You may not be able to return to the Pulpit right now, but you are still in ministry right here on Facebook." Another shared: "Take heart my friend…God is in control. May He comfort and strengthen you." One last note: "Pastor, I don't want you suffering, but thank you for pointing me to my loving, all powerful, Shepherd King." I could include other testimonials that have been sent and spoken of their great appreciation for my interest in their life and need. One very touching communication was from a man who had drifted and wandered from the Lord for more than fifty years and has returned to Him by God's marvelous grace.

The "Tribe of Barnabas" – may it increase with those who genuinely love and care for others, step forward, stand in the gap, run any risk, and be an encourager and/or consoler to and for others. May God richly bless you as you wear that mantle for the glory of God alone.

11. Inexcusable

There are always situations and circumstances where choices must be made. Obviously, the choice between right and wrong is always one of the choices. Paul was frank and on-point when he wrote (Romans 1:18-31 – NLT):

> God shows his anger from heaven against all sinful, wicked people who suppress the truth by their wickedness. They know the truth about God because he has made it obvious to them…They have no excuse for not knowing God. Yes, they knew God, but they wouldn't worship him as God or even give him thanks…
>
> Since they thought it foolish to acknowledge God, he abandoned them to their foolish thinking and let them do things that should never be done. Their lives became full of every kind of wickedness, sin, greed, hate, envy, murder, quarreling, deception, malicious behavior, and gossip. They are backstabbers, haters of God, insolent, proud, and boastful. They invent new ways of sinning, and they disobey their parents. They refuse to understand, break their promises, are heartless, and have no mercy. They know God's justice requires that those who do these things deserve to die, yet they do them anyway. Worse yet, they encourage others to do them, too.

The clear Word from God to the wicked is clear: "They have no excuse for not knowing God." In a very similar way, there is clarity in terms of how the Biblical Christian is to live, know and do. In like manner, they are without excuse if the Word of God is ignored or not applied. In a Devotional by Charles Swindoll on June 5, 2020, he wrote on the subject of Choosing God's Will. He wrote:

> A major goal of wholesome, healthy Christians is the hope of reaching maturity before death overtakes us. I will tell you without hesitation that one of my major goals in life is to grow up as I grow older. A commendable etching on a gravestone would be: Here lies a man who kept growing as he kept aging. Growing up and growing old need to walk hand in hand. Never doubt it: maturing is a slow, arduous process...
>
> As Oswald Chambers wrote: 'To choose suffering makes no sense at all; to choose God's will in the midst of our suffering makes all the sense in the world.' Where are you today? Where is your journey leading you? More important, which option have you chosen? Are you viewing your trial as an outrage or an opportunity?

Two of the Questions posed above are: "Where are you today? Where is your journey leading you?" How does the Biblical Christian answer these questions before the Holy

11. Inexcusable

God? Do we offer God our excuses or our repentance and contrition? When His Word states (Micah 6:8 – NLT): "O people, the LORD has told you what is good, and this is what he requires of you: to do what is right, to love mercy, and to walk humbly with your God." In our daily walk before and with our Lord, are we always doing what is right; are we always loving and showing mercy; are we always walking humbly with our God? Yikes! This is so unequivocal and clear. It Leaves me in the shadow of His declaration: This is unacceptable and inexcusable! It causes me to think of a very old Hymn translated by John Wesley. The beginning words are: "What Shall I Offer To The Lord?" Isaac Watts wrote a Hymn that begins with a poignant question: "What shall I render to my God For all His kindness shown?"

In a Facebook entry, Steve Sellers wrote:

> When is the last time you let the following know you appreciate them, your spouse, parents, grandparents, children, friends, teacher, pastor, staff member of your church, employees, employer, waitress, neighbor and you can add to the list. Amazing how just telling someone you appreciate them and what they do brings the cool breeze of encouragement over the one(s) to whom you spoke words of appreciation.

As I was writing this paragraph (June 17, 2020), my Barnabas friend (Steve Sellers) sent me a note: Praying for you!

James Perry

> Does Jesus care when my heart is pained
> Too deeply for mirth and song;
> As the burdens press and cares distress,
> And the way grows weary and long?

Refrain:
> Oh Yes, He Cares—I Know He Cares!
> His heart is touched with My Grief;
> When the Days are Weary,
> the Long Nights Dreary,
> I know My Savior Cares.

These words lifted my spirit and caused me to rejoice. Do you know someone who would benefit similarly with just a word of care? Could you give someone you know a spiritual nudge to remind the person you contact that Jesus does indeed care?

There are three passages to consider in terms of the inexcusable or genuinely acceptable. First is Romans 12:1-2 – ESV),

> I appeal to you… brothers and sisters, by the mercies of God, to present your bodies as a living sacrifice, holy and ACCEPTABLE to God, which is your spiritual worship. Do not be conformed to this world, but be transformed by the renewal of your mind, that by testing you may discern what is the will of God, what is good and ACCEPTABLE and perfect.

11. Inexcusable

In terms of God's will, is your commitment before God acceptable or unacceptable?

Second is Romans 15:5-7 (NIV):

> May the God who gives endurance and encouragement give you the same attitude of mind toward each other that Christ Jesus had, so that with one mind and one voice you may glorify the God and Father of our Lord Jesus Christ. ACCEPT one another, then, just as Christ ACCEPTED you, in order to bring praise to God.

Is this how we consider one another before God? Have we allowed ourselves to fall into the snare of being overly-selective in terms of who we accept or reject? Do we accept others unconditionally? That's how Jesus Christ accepted us who are His children and followers.

Third is Ephesians 4:31-32 (NIV):

> Get rid of all bitterness, rage and anger, brawling and slander, along with every form of malice. Be kind and compassionate to one another, forgiving each other, just as in Christ God forgave you.

Why should one get rid of the things God is aggrieved by? Answer: Ephesians 4:30 (NLT): "Do not bring sorrow to God's Holy Spirit by the way you live." The other response is that the Biblical Christian is to forgive others in the same manner God has forgiven in Jesus Christ – unconditionally.

In Matthew 6:11 (NLT): This is how Jesus instructed His disciples and all other followers to pray and do – "Forgive us our sins, as we have forgiven those who sin against us." Is this the way we consistently forgive others – unconditionally and the same way Jesus has forgiven those who believe? Each of us knows the emphatic answer! It is – Yes!

A Hymn written in 1851 by Arthur T. Russell indicates the words Jesus offered to the Heavenly Father:

> Forgive, O Father! Jesus cries;
> Lord, may Thy prayer for us arise;
> Cleanse us from our transgression:
> Our guilt Thou knowest—Thou alone;
> Accept, Lord, our confession.

Another Hymn written in 1875 by Cecil F. Alexander widened the horizon in terms of forgiveness when he wrote:

> For me was that compassion,
> For me that tender care;
> I need His wide forgiveness
> As much as any there.
> It was my pride and hardness
> That hung Him on the tree;
> Those cruel nails, O Savior,
> Were driven in by me.

11. Inexcusable

May our Lord and Savior find us and our actions to be genuinely acceptable before Him. May His will be our greatest desire as we pursue A Barnabas Quest. The Lord needs us to be compassionate and accepting of others for Him. Can he count on you to be a Barnabas-type for Him? If so, He will be pleased and you will be blest!

12. Underestimation

There are unguarded times when underestimating or miscalculating the power and authority of God occurs. Those who are Biblical Christians are careful in this area but the subtle moments we all experience allows for the questions: Where is God when all of this is happening? Why does God not intervene when the evil appears to be gaining victories that are detrimental to the righteous? Who's in charge of world events and the direction of the culture in which one resides?

Hopefully, the words of Scripture will remind us that God is always in control and His power is never diminished. Psalm 46:1-3 (NIV) reminds us: "God is our refuge and strength, an ever-present help in trouble. Therefore we will not fear, though the earth give way and the mountains fall into the heart of the sea, though its waters roar and foam and the mountains quake with their surging." Psalm 86:9-12 (NIV) reminds us: "All the nations you have made will come and worship before you, Lord; they will bring glory to your name. For you are great and do marvelous deeds; you alone are God. Teach me your way, LORD, that I may rely on your faithfulness; give me an undivided heart, that I may fear your name. I will praise you, Lord my God, with all my heart; I will glorify your name forever."

When I was engaged in a more pastoral-oriented ministry, I would try to discover a person's favorite passage (or passages) of Scripture. I did this for several reasons, not the least of which was how well a person read and understood the Bible, and what had special meaning for them as a child of God. Many times, I received the answer – Psalm 23 or John 3:16. It was very refreshing when there were more -in-depth responses. I visited with an older woman who knew death was getting closer. When I asked which verse in the Bible meant the most to her, without hesitation she recited Second Timothy 1:7 (NKJV), "For God has not given us a spirit of fear, but of power and of love and of a sound mind." She did two things that were meaningful. She personalized the text and said: "God has not given ME a spirit of fear." When she came to the last phrase she paused momentarily, then she pointed to her forehead and said "a sound mind." It was a special and unforgettable moment. She did not – had not – underestimated the power and authority of her Lord and Savior. Not too long after that time with her, she died and I had the privilege of officiating at her funeral. In case you were wondering, the brief homily was based upon Second Timothy 1:7. "God has not given ME a spirit of fear, but of power and of love and of a sound mind."

Anyone with a commitment to faithfully follow the Lord will experience times of challenge by the forces of evil. Paul was very explicit when he emphasized the spiritual opposition one will be exposed to while doing good in the name of Jesus. Paul emphasized that the whole armor of God was necessary if the one serving the Lord was to survive (Ephesians 6:10-20 – NIV). Some of his instruction includes the reason for the armor requirement:

12. Underestimation

Be strong in the Lord and in his mighty power. Put on the full armor of God, so that you can take your stand against the devil's schemes. For our struggle is not against flesh and blood, but against the rulers, against the authorities, against the powers of this dark world and against the spiritual forces of evil in the heavenly realms. Therefore put on the full armor of God, so that when the day of evil comes, you may be able to stand your ground, and after you have done everything, to stand.

Paul emphasizes "the mighty power of God" for the servants of the Lord when they oppose and engage against the powers of this dark world. It would be foolish to reach a conclusion about who is the primary instigator of opposition to the ministry of the Lord Jesus Christ. While the primary instigator is always Satan and his minions, there are other factors that can become overwhelming. Psychological, emotional, being trapped in the murmuring and complaining syndrome – can become the tools used by "The Instigator". If the whole armor of God is secured by each one, it will matter little who or what the opposition is or from what direction it will come. One area of great need of the mighty power of God is combating the increasing suicide rates in this nation as well as in the world. The more common causes of suicide as determined by the Centers For Disease Control (CDC) are:

Many suicides are the result of circumstances that were beyond avoidable. One thing that is a heavy commonality among people who die by suicide is an unshakeable feeling of dread, despair, loneliness, and hopelessness. These adjectives can be said to be overused in the discussions revolving around suicide, but they need to be taken seriously in order for suicide rates by state to decrease.

This makes the need of A Barnabas Quest all the more viable. A dear man of God recently shared with me the following: "Today a Pastor is about to throw in the towel. Your phone call or visit as a fellow servant to encourage and love him can make a difference in his life." Please read this sentence once again. There may be someone you know or who is within the horizon of your life that needs and could use a special word of encouragement; Biblical truth; prayer – or – maybe taking the person out for a meal.

There are various aspects of ministry that can become burdensome. Those serving in ministry may begin to get the feeling that no one really cares about what is being done anyway. Whether it is done or not done, who really cares? Everyone seems to be caught up in their own world of interests – family, employment, education, aging, etc. It is important that one assess his/her priorities. If one is too busy to show interest in another's cares or burdens, that one is too, too busy and has embraced an incorrect choice of priorities.

What should you and I embrace for our individual lives regarding the capacity we have to minister to the lives and needs of others? If there is a personal desire to be effective

12. Underestimation

and productive, the power of God will make that a reality in one's life. There are many relevant passages of Scripture that one should embrace but two I suggest as a beginning point are:

> Second Peter 1:3-8 – NIV, His divine power has given us everything we need for a godly life through our knowledge of him who called us by his own glory and goodness. Through these he has given us his very great and precious promises, so that through them you may participate in the divine nature, having escaped the corruption in the world caused by evil desires. For this very reason, make every effort to add to your faith goodness; and to goodness, knowledge; and to knowledge, self-control; and to self-control, perseverance; and to perseverance, godliness; and to godliness, mutual affection; and to mutual affection, love. For if you possess these qualities in increasing measure, they will keep you from being ineffective and unproductive in your knowledge of our Lord Jesus Christ.

> Ephesians 3:20-21 – (NIV), Now to him who is able to do immeasurably more than all we ask or imagine, according to his power that is at work within us, to him be glory in the church and in Christ Jesus throughout all generations, for ever and ever! Amen.

Both of these passages reference the divine power and authority that is given to every child of God who is willing to receive it. The God who has called us to represent Him in this eroding world expects us to remember His power and authority. We should also join in worship and praise as we sing to Him - - -

> Our God is an awesome God
> He reigns from heaven above
> With wisdom, power, and love
> Our God is an awesome God.

> What a mighty God we serve…
> Angels bow before him.
> Heaven and earth adore him.
> What a mighty God we serve.

13. Prayerfulness

The Westminster Shorter Catechism asks: What is Prayer? The answer: "Prayer is an offering up of our desires unto God, for things agreeable to his will, in the name of Christ, with confession of our sins, and thankful acknowledgment of his mercies." A foundational basis for prayer is given in Psalm 62:1, 8 (NKJV): "Truly my soul silently waits for God; from Him comes my salvation (victory)…Trust in Him at all times, you people; Pour out your heart before Him; God is a refuge for us…" If one is in doubt about how one should pray and that for which one should request, the book of Psalms contains varying subjects to guide one in prayer. To do an in-depth study of the book of Psalms, one would be well-served by utilizing the Treasury of David by C. H. Spurgeon.

The general subject material in the book of Psalms includes the types of prayers that were offered: Prayers of Thanksgiving; Supplication; Intercessory; Imprecatory; Messianic; Corporate/Public; Closet/Private; Worship; Consecration; Faith. The idea conveyed: Prayer is basic communication with God. The list could easily become longer. A cautionary word is that one should not just select one basic form/manner for praying but comprehend that prayer is all-encompassing. As one Prays, perspicacity is an important factor. One must pray with "keenness of mental perception and understanding; discernment; penetration." Prayer is serious communication with the Holy God who has indicated in His Word (Jeremiah 33:3 – ESV): "Call to me and I will answer you, and will tell you great and hidden things that you have not known." There must be a whole-hearted commitment to the Lord as and when one prays (Jeremiah 29:13 – ESV): "You will seek me and find me, when you seek me with all your heart." The MSG expresses this verse: "When you come looking for me, you'll find me. Yes, when you get serious about finding me and want it more than anything else, I'll make sure you won't be disappointed."

A primary guideline for prayer is given in Philippians 4:6-7 (NKJV) and is useful for one who is committed to prayer:

> Be anxious for nothing, but in everything by prayer and supplication, with thanksgiving, let your requests be made known to God; and the peace of God, which surpasses all understanding, will guard your hearts and minds through Jesus Christ.

In the NLT, the opening words are: "Don't worry about anything; instead, pray about everything…" When one prays, is there a possibility of error in the subject matter of the prayer? Yes! However, there is a provision granted by the Lord via the Holy Spirit to review the words one is expressing in prayer. There is never an authorization to commune with God recklessly or thoughtlessly. One should never pray about the success of a crime – arson; murder; assassination; fraud; theft; kidnapping; etc.

13. Prayerfulness

As a safeguard for God's people as they pray, the words of Romans 8:26-27 (ESV) are terse but assuring:

> The Holy Spirit helps us in our weakness. For we do not know what to pray for as we ought, but the Holy Spirit himself intercedes for us with groanings too deep for words. And he who searches hearts knows what is the mind of the Holy Spirit, because the Holy Spirit intercedes for the saints according to the will of God.

An important caution about Prayer was given by Jesus Christ after His disciples asked Him to teach them to Pray. Matthew 6:5-8 (ESV):

> When you pray, you must not be like the hypocrites. For they love to stand and pray in the synagogues and at the street corners, that they may be seen by others. Truly, I say to you, they have received their reward. But when you pray, go into your room and shut the door and pray to your Father who is in secret. And your Father who sees in secret will reward you. And when you pray, do not heap up empty phrases as the Gentiles do, for they think that they will be heard for their many words. Do not be like them, for your Father knows what you need before you ask him.

These words of Jesus Christ could eliminate much of the verbalization that is stated aloud in both public and private praying. At times, some prayers sound more like developed orations. In those cases, the prayer may impress assembled people but the idea of prayer is to express from one's heart the worship God desires and the cares he permits one to make known to Him. Prayer must always have the Lord in focus. This may be a reason why Jesus instructed in Matthew 6:6 (NIV), "When you pray, go into your room, close the door and pray to your Father, who is unseen. Then your Father, who sees what is done in secret, will reward you (openly)."

God was never impressed by the words offered by the hypocrites. Who were they trying to impress – God or man? What was their goal – group affirmation or a Holy God's intervention/interceding? The Lord has no place for the words, actions and intentions of the hypocrites. Jesus denounces the behavior of the hypocrites in Matthew 23 where He pronounces His woes upon the scribes and Pharisees.

James 5:13-16 (ESV), there is a recommendation for transparency among those sharing a like-precious faith. The statement made by James is not exhaustive but is practical in terms of basic human need:

> Is anyone among you suffering? Let him pray. Is anyone cheerful? Let him sing praise. Is anyone among you sick? Let him call for the elders of the church, and let them pray over him, anointing him with oil in the name of the Lord. And the prayer of faith will save the

13. Prayerfulness

one who is sick, and the Lord will raise him up. And if he has committed sins, he will be forgiven. Therefore, confess your sins to one another and pray for one another, that you may be healed. The prayer of a righteous person has great power as it is working.

The area of Prayer requires authenticity both for the one(s) who pray as well as on the part of the one requesting prayer. There should never be attempts to fake it before God or to present artificial factors as genuine requests. Jeremiah 17:9-10 (NKJV) reminds all that:

> The heart is deceitful above all things and is desperately wicked; who can know it? I, the LORD, search the heart, I test the mind, even to give every man, woman, child according to his ways, according to the fruit of his doings (actions and deeds).

The one desiring to be used by God as a Barnabas servant is required to be a person of prayer. My friend who prays regularly for me, also prays similarly for several others as they labor for the Lord. To each of us, he makes time to share a personal word of hope and encouragement. He will soon retire (January 2021) from the Children's Home ministry that he loves and has served for many years. He will be missed by the children and also in the church where he represents the need and ministry of The Children's Home. There is room for others to stand in that gap with him. Can you be counted on to become a faithful Barnabas who will care and share the burdens of others?

In 1818, James Montgomery was moved to write a Hymn with the title: Prayer Is The Soul's Sincere Desire. Some of the stanzas include:

> Prayer is the soul's sincere desire,
> Unuttered or expressed;
> The motion of a hidden fire
> That trembles in the breast.
>
> The saints in prayer appear as one
> In word, in deed, and mind,
> While with the Father and the Son
> Sweet fellowship they find.
> Nor prayer is made on earth alone;
> The Holy Spirit pleads,
> And Jesus, on the eternal throne,
> For sinners intercedes.

14. Quitting

Every year hundreds and thousands of pastors and ancillary church personnel from most denominations wrestle with and ultimately choose to leave ministry. Some of the major reasons are disappointment, distress and depression. Other reasons include individual personality factors and clashes, as well as conflict with the strong natural leaders within an organization. I have seen it firsthand in the twenty-first century church. It is easy to wonder "why" people quit attending some of these churches. They leave quietly and never return. I have seen church bulletins where a prayer list includes: "Pray that our church will grow and impact our community." The prayer goes unanswered. Why? The prayer listing is incorrect! It should read: "Keep us from dominating the local church effort where "my/our" will dominates and God's will is not actually sought." Having this prayer answered will require certain individuals to humble himself/herself and to repent of a dominating spirit that is evil at its core and harmful as it persists.

Several years ago, I attended a minister's conference where the principal speaker was Dr. Howard Hendricks (a Dallas Theological Seminary Professor at that time). He addressed the subject: What Does It Take To Make You Want To Quit? His general concern was who a person is in relationship to Jesus Christ and His authority. He made many pithy comments over the years of his own ministry. One of them was: "My great concern for you in life is not that you will fail, but that you will succeed in doing the wrong things." This was attached to the priority that should exist within each one whom God has called into ministry. It is reminding oneself often about the call and will of God for one's life. Hendricks often said: "Every disciple needs three types of relationships in his life. He needs a 'Paul' who can mentor him and challenge him. He needs a 'Barnabas' who can come along side and encourage him. And he needs a 'Timothy,' someone that he can pour his life into."

Reflect on these three priorities. Focus upon: "He needs a 'Barnabas' who can come along side and encourage him." The application of this comment is obvious. This is sometimes called mentoring. Mentoring can be invaluable and its worth should be understood by those in ministry, especially by those newly ordained. Some of these new ministers may be under the false impression that they have "arrived" following their graduation from Seminary and receiving approval from an ecclesiastical body that has ordained them into ministry. They need to realize that their journey is just beginning and they need to seek a mentor from the more experienced and mature man/men for input into their life and ministry.

Paul exercised a mentoring ministry by writing letters to younger men such as his letters to Timothy and Titus. There was also his effort with Philemon regarding slavery and his relationship to and treatment of the runaway slave. In several instances, Paul's letters to the churches were also mentoring exhortations. To the Church at Philippi, his letter (mentoring)

14. Quitting

was reflective of a Barnabas where he encouraged the people. To the Church in Galatia his mentoring was more confrontational because of the influx of legalism within the church. In one of his letters to Timothy, he notes those who had quit the ministry and opted to doing other things.

There is an interesting Scriptural comparison of the usage and meaning of "quit" when facing an opponent as opposed to just walking away from the challenge. There is a scene in First Samuel 4:8-9 (KJV) where Israel had been in a battle with the Philistines and had 4,000 casualties. The elders of Israel told the disheartened troops that they need to go to Shiloh and bring the Ark of the Covenant into the midst of their battle. They did so. When the Ark of the Covenant appeared, the enthusiastic shouts of Israel caused the ground to tremble. The Philistines concluded they were unable to fight against the God of Israel. However, the Philistine leaders incited their troops: "Be strong, and quit yourselves like men, O ye Philistines, that ye be not servants unto the Hebrews, as they have been to you: quit yourselves like men, and fight" (KJV). The NLT captures the intent and meaning of the leader's challenge: "Fight as never before, Philistines! If you don't, we will become the Hebrews' slaves just as they have been ours! Stand up like men and fight!" The word "quit" was not intended to have the Philistines surrender. It was a call to have courage and to take the battle to Israel. When they did, Israel lost another 30,000 men in the battle and the Ark of the Covenant was seized by the Philistines.

Fast forward to First Corinthians 16:13 (KJV) where Paul is giving some final exhortations which include: "Watch ye, stand fast in the faith, quit you like men, be strong." Other translations word it: (ESV) "Be watchful, stand firm in the faith, act like men, be strong." In the NLT, the thought is expressed to mean: "Be on guard. Stand firm in the faith. Be courageous. Be strong." Paul is stressing the need and place for the whole armor of God. He also emphasizes the vicious attacks of the devil and spiritual forces in high places. He echoes the Philistine words of First Samuel 4 when he states in Ephesians 6:11 (ESV): "Be on guard. Stand firm in the faith. Be courageous. Be strong." Paul never thought of or suggested that one should "quit" or surrender to the enemy, opposition or spiritual forces. He never deviated from the ministry types that were and are sorely needed: "'Paul' who can mentor and challenge... A 'Barnabas' who can come along side and encourage... A 'Timothy' who can and will can pour his life into another. The thrust is always present – do not quit! There is much the Lord wants His people to be and do.

> When the evil one comes against you,
> To fill your heart with fear;
> You can trust in God He will never leave you,
> He promised to be near.
> You can lift up a song In the midst of the war,
> For the battle is mine says the Lord!

15. Action

Action or inaction is the question for the Biblical Christian and the Evangelical Church in the twenty-first century. When Peter wrote his epistles, he established particular guidelines for the people who were being persecuted and scattered. What should one do when the foundations of faith are rumbling and some crumbling? How should the Biblical Christian interact with the culture that is moving closer to godlessness? Is there any way for one to be prepared adequately for the changing times in which one is living? When a Biblical Christian is isolated from his/her church and support groups, is there an impact one can continue to make in the lives of others? What is the initial counsel Peter states to the people?

First Peter 1:13-19 emphasizes that one should not shift one's mind into neutral but into action-orientation. In the various translations of the Bible utilized by people in the church community, there is clarity in why one's behavior must continue to be uncompromised. Peter writes: "Prepare your minds for action and be sober-minded." The NIV translates the verse: "With minds that are alert and fully sober." In J. B. Phillips: "Brace up your minds and… know what you are doing." In the MSG, there is a comprehensive summation regarding one's faithfulness to his/her commitment to Jesus Christ:

So roll up your sleeves, put your mind in gear, be totally ready to receive the gift that's coming when Jesus arrives. Don't lazily slip back into those old grooves of evil, doing just what you feel like doing.

There is a further obligation indicated in Verse 12 (ESV): "As he who called you is holy, you also be holy in all your conduct." Personal holiness is a work of gradual development. It is carried on under many hindrances, hence the frequent admonitions to watchfulness, prayer, and perseverance. Paul is direct and forceful when he wrote the Church at Ephesus (Ephesians 4:22-24 – NLT): "Throw off your old sinful nature and your former way of life, which is corrupted by lust and deception. Instead, let the Spirit renew your thoughts and attitudes. Put on your new nature, created to be like God - truly righteous and holy." When Paul addressed this subject in Second Corinthians 7:1 (NLT), he did so against the backdrop of Second Corinthians 6:14-18 regarding one being a temple of the Living God. As such, the expected behavioral commitment is: "Because we have these promises…let us cleanse ourselves from everything that can defile our body or spirit. And let us work toward complete holiness because we fear God."

When Jerry Bridges wrote and published his book, The Pursuit of Holiness, the foundation for his brilliant work is based on: "God has called every Christian to a holy life. There are no exceptions to this call." Howard Hendricks adds: "Spend the rest of your life doing what God prepared you to

15. Action

do." Why is this application of holiness in one's life important? In the New Living Translation, there is a paragraph heading: "A Call to Listen to God." What is that call? What should the Biblical Christian listen to, hear and apply? What ensuing action is both required and expected? We find an answer in Hebrews 12:14-16 (NLT): "Work at living in peace with everyone, and work at living a holy life, for those who are not holy will not see the Lord. Look after each other so that none of you fails to receive the grace of God. Watch out that no poisonous root of bitterness grows up to trouble you, corrupting many."

There are four minimal areas of living out God's call given in this passage:

(1) Work at living in peace with everyone
(2) Work at living a Holy life
(3) Work at looking after each other
(4) Work at Watching that no poisonous root of bitterness grows up in your life and midst

Jerry Bridges adds:

> We need to pray daily for humility and honesty to see these sinful attitudes for what they really are, and then for grace and discipline to root them out of our minds and replace them with thoughts pleasing to God.

He elaborates on some of the required actions for the Biblical Christian:

> We need to brace ourselves up and realize that we are responsible for thoughts, attitudes, and actions. We need to reckon on the fact that we died to sin's reign, that it no longer has any dominion over us, that God has united us with the risen Christ in all His power and has given us the Holy Spirit to work in us. Only as we accept our responsibility and appropriate God's provisions will we make any progress in our pursuit of holiness.

Do these actions represent who and what you are? Is your life making any difference in the life of others? Are you actively engaged with some who are needy, oppressed, downcast, overwhelmed by the cares of this life? How can one's actions be measured? I am convicted as I read the Olivet Discourse when Jesus addresses this area of action or inaction in one's life-choices. Matthew 25:31-46 is the grim assessment of actions and inactions as it relates to the final judgment. These verses suggest that the meaning Jesus Christ has attached to a disciple's life should never be trifled with or ignored. A casual approach to life in general will allow one to have a casual approach to the things that are a concern of Jesus Christ and will eventually lead to inaction. The difference is between commitment and indifference.

15. Action

The Hebrews 12 passage addressed "work at" looking after each other. In Matthew 25, Jesus establishes the heavenly parameters of what "work at" looking after each other means. The subject in the Olivet Discourse is the distinction made between sheep who listen to the shepherd's call and goats who don't. In some detail, Jesus addresses what it means to look after the interests of others. In verses 35-36, Jesus personalizes the areas of need he is defining. He said to the sheep:

> Come, you who are blessed by My Father, inherit the kingdom…I was hungry, and you fed me. I was thirsty, and you gave me a drink. I was a stranger, and you invited me into your home. I was naked, and you gave me clothing. I was sick, and you cared for me. I was in prison, and you visited me.

This is a checklist of the basic needs that confront people every day. Jesus knows the thoughts, words and deeds of both the sheep and the goats. He measures how both the sheep and goats respond to human needs. What do the sheep and goats know, see and do? The sheep are measured by Jesus and were found to have responded actively, caringly and with compassion. The goats respond from their indifference saying that if they had really seen or known of the needs, they would've responded accordingly. In the case of the goats, the indifference is now coupled with insincerity. There is an eternal result in the balance. The sheep hear: "Come and inherit the kingdom prepared for you from the creation of the world. You, the righteous will enter into eternal life." The goats hear: "You will go away to eternal punishment."

A Hymn titled: God Who Spoke In The Beginning, has these lines in one of the stanzas:

> Christ– calls us to a life of service,
> Heart and will to action stirred...

Is this your song, commitment, and observable behavior? As you prepare your mind and will for action, God will give you opportunities to put your talent(s) into use for His kingdom purposes. There is a need for those who will seek and commit to be a Barnabas for the lives and needs of others. Will you pursue The Barnabas Quest? There is a place and room for you to do so! You should yield to Jesus Christ today and find the true meaning of holiness, righteousness and blessing as you obediently walk with Him and actively serve Him.

16. Overcoming

Have you ever been in a situation where distrust, fear, ostracization, isolation, rebellion are real factors regarding another person, or maybe about you? What should you do if you disbelieve another's changed life? Do you agree with the majority opinion or do you step forward and endeavor to make a difference on behalf of another? What if the disbelief is about your changed life - do you cringe and slip away into obscurity or do you endeavor to gain acceptance by anyone or everyone?

Two incidents from scripture come to mind which illustrate disbelief in people. The first occasion is found in Numbers 13 and 14. Moses had been directed by the Lord to send twelve spies into the land of Canaan and to report their findings upon their return. Ten of the spies gave a mixed report. They indicated the land was fruitful but impossible to conquer. They spoke about the appearance of very large people living there and summarized by saying: "We seemed to ourselves like grasshoppers, and so we seemed to them" (Numbers 13:32-33). This was a disturbing and bad report to both Moses and the Israelites. The people were upset upon hearing the majority report. They began to murmur among themselves and complain bitterly to Moses. What could Moses do in this situation? Should he suggest they attempt to build a community in the desert? Should they return to Egypt and seek Pharaoh's reinstatement?

Before that kind of decision can be made, there is a minority who have a positive and encouraging report. Despite the people's thought that they should dispose of Moses as their leader, Joshua and Caleb step forward with an optimistic declaration (Numbers 14:6-9, ESV). They sought the attention of all the people and then said:

> The land, which we passed through to spy it out, is an exceedingly good land. If the LORD delights in us, he will bring us into this land and give it to us, a land that flows with milk and honey. Only do not rebel against the LORD. And do not fear the people of the land, for they are bread for us. Their protection is removed from them, and the LORD is with us; do not fear them.

What will the people do with this alternative report? Will they say among themselves: "Whew! We're glad Joshua and Caleb set the record straight! This is the news we've been waiting to hear. At long last, we will gain our own homeland. Praise the Lord!" No! That was not their response! Instead, the response was absurdly negative: "The whole community began to talk about stoning Joshua and Caleb." Why would two spies have such a remarkable alternative report? It was said of them, Numbers 32:12 (NLT), "The only exceptions are Caleb and Joshua…for they have wholeheartedly followed the LORD."

When taking an unpopular position among an incensed group of people, one can face challenges and threats. What

16. Overcoming

will it take to get the people led by Moses to respond affirmatively? Nothing. The end of this account reports that all who rebelled died in the wilderness and never saw The Promised Land that the Lord wanted them to have, conquer and enjoy. Only Joshua and Caleb, along with the second generation of Israelites would enter The Promised Land but it would take forty-years waiting for the first generation to die before that would be realized.

There is a comparable New Testament report that stirs up a group of people. Saul of Tarsus was representing the religious leadership and authorities of his day with letters of persecution against anyone embracing the Gospel of the Lord Jesus Christ. The Jesus Christ followers knew one thing about this man - he was a threat to their worship practices and their beliefs, as well as to their lives. Acts 9:1-2 (ESV) summarizes Saul's ambitions:

> Saul, still breathing threats and murder against the disciples of the Lord, went to the high priest and asked him for letters to the synagogues at Damascus, so that if he found any belonging to the Way, men or women, he might bring them bound to Jerusalem.

His goal was to eliminate the Christians existence. How can the people overcome this threat and opposition? Should they flee or stand their ground? Will they be willing to die, to become martyrs, for the things they had come to believe? Who can come to their rescue?

Acts 9 relates a very important intrusion into this determined man's plan. The people did not calculate divine intervention on their behalf. They had no knowledge of God's will and plan for Saul's future. While on the road with letters of persecution, Saul was struck to the ground by a great and very bright light. He was blinded. Saul heard a voice addressing him by name (Acts 9:4-6, ESV): "Saul, why are you persecuting me? I am Jesus, whom you are persecuting. Rise and enter the city, and you will be told what you are to do." Saul cannot see and was led by the hand into Damascus. He goes three days unable to see and without food or beverage. An intervention and change of direction was about to occur. A man named Ananias was directed to go to Saul and intervene for the Lord. Despite a natural fear about what he was directed to do, the Lord assures him of the divine change that will take place in the dreaded Saul from Tarsus. The Lord indicates to Ananias, Acts 9:15-16, "Go, for he is a chosen instrument of mine to carry my name before the Gentiles and kings and the children of Israel. For I will show him how much he must suffer for the sake of my name."

Saul had no idea what was going to take place in his life and future. He would learn that not only would his life be transformed but the mission he was ambitiously carrying out would also be redefined. His letters of persecution would be set aside and he would soon have letters for the churches that he would help establish. Letters to the church at Rome, Galatia, Ephesus, Philippi, Colossi as well as personal letters to Timothy, Titus, Philemon. He would fearlessly speak before

16. Overcoming

kings and church leaders. He would represent Jesus Christ boldly and courageously.

Would the existing Christian community willingly and eagerly receive this transformed persecutor into their lives and fellowship? Would you? Would you believe that God's work of grace could redeem this ruthless opponent and threat? Before answering the questions, consider those who you are inadvertently holding at arm's length and not enthusiastically embracing or willingly accepting into your fellowship. Would you trust such a one? Would you stand alongside and help that one know more about the Lord? Would you mentor and encourage this person to grow in the grace and knowledge of the Lord Jesus Christ? Do you have self-imposed restrictions based upon the declaration and description of certain cultural behaviors? Consider the transformation in Saul (now Paul). Would you understand and apply First Corinthians 6:9-11 (NLT).

> Don't you realize that those who do wrong will not inherit the Kingdom of God? Don't fool yourselves. Those who indulge in sexual sin, or who worship idols, or commit adultery, or are male prostitutes, or practice homosexuality, or are thieves, or greedy people, or drunkards, or are abusive, or cheat people - none of these will inherit the Kingdom of God. Some of you were once like that.

This would also include the one who persecutes those who believe and proclaim the Gospel of Jesus Christ. Before jumping to a judgmental conclusion, read and reread, underscore and enlarge the words: "Some of you were once like that." Whoa! That can't be true! Not me! Before trying to defend oneself, understand why your life has been transformed and why you are now a new person in Jesus Christ. The text continues: "But you were cleansed; you were made holy; you were made right with God by calling on the name of the Lord Jesus Christ and by the Spirit of our God."

The response about accepting one whose life had been changed, in Saul's day, was a suspicious and emphatic "No!" Was there anyone who would or could come to his side and convince others that this man's transformation was real and sincere? What should one do when a plot to kill Saul was being circulated? A very few helped him to escape but he remained unacceptable to the majority of true believers in Jesus Christ. Acts 9:26 records: "When Saul arrived in Jerusalem, he tried to meet with the believers, but they were all afraid of him. They did not believe he had truly become a believer!"

The words upon which this book is based is a phrase found in Acts 9:27, "But Barnabas." There was one man willing to risk everything to come to the defense of a transformed convert to the Christian way of life. What else would Barnabas do? The text continues: "Barnabas brought him to the apostles and told them how Saul had seen the Lord on the way to Damascus and how the Lord had spoken to Saul. He

16. Overcoming

also told them that Saul had preached boldly in the name of Jesus in Damascus." Would anyone else stand alongside Barnabas and accept this convert? The apostles trusted Barnabas and let Saul stay with them (Acts 9:28), "So Saul stayed with the apostles and went all around Jerusalem with them, preaching boldly in the name of the Lord." All because of a Barnabas.

> At the sign of triumph Satan's host doth flee;
> On then, Christian soldiers, on to victory.
> Hell's foundations quiver at the shout of praise,
> Brothers lift your voices, loud your anthems raise.
>
> Like a mighty army moves the church of God.
> Brothers, we are treading where the saints have trod.
> We are not divided, all one body we
> One in hope and doctrine, one in charity.
>
> Onward, Christian Soldiers.

17. Resolute

What if there had not been a Barnabas intervention? Who would've stepped forward on behalf of Saul of Tarsus? In the experiences of life today, who takes a stand on behalf of one who is marginalized or ostracized? How often have you intervened for another – an acquaintance; a family member; when an injustice is occurring? Would you be willing to intervene as Barnabas did for Saul?

On June 22, 2020, Charles Swindoll wrote about the effectiveness of Barnabas in the Devotional, Insight For Today (Acts 9:27). "The disciples feared Saul. They couldn't bring themselves to believe he was a disciple. 'But Barnabas…' Isn't that a great opening? Out of nowhere comes Barnabas to encourage Saul and be his personal advocate." In a way, this is how Steve and I became friends and he became my Barnabas – out of nowhere came Steve – in an hour of when I heard I was Stage 4 with Lymphoma. In the case of Barnabas and Saul, a broader question raised asks: "How did Barnabas know Saul needed his help? We don't know." The issue is whether or not someone has an inner sense of an acceptable stand to take on behalf of another. The choice and decision made by a potential Barnabas is whether or not one will run the risk on behalf of one who needs help and encouragement.

Swindoll writes: "…we do know that God is sovereign and has his Barnabas in every town, every church, on every college and seminary campus, and even on the mission field.

Each Barnabas stands ready at a moment's notice to come to the aid of someone in need of encouragement." Is that a correct assumption or some wishful thinking? Have you ever wished for a Barnabas to be available for you? Have you ever considered being a Barnabas for someone else?

Sometimes we offer Scriptural counsel to a troubled, or gravely ill, or needy person. A verse that is often quoted (usually out of context) is First Peter 5:7 (NLT), "Give all your worries and cares to God, for he cares about you." Another verse that is similar appears in Psalm 55:22 (NLT), "Give your burdens to the LORD, and he will take care of you. He will not permit the godly to slip and fall." Both passages are valid for one's peace in the midst of turmoil and comfort amid uncertainty.

Barnabas was a person of action. He saw a need and responded immediately. He knew the fear and prejudice that prevailed but he also discerned what was right in God's sight. Barnabas stepped up and put his arm of encouragement around Saul. Saul was willing to accept his assistance. Essentially, the action of Barnabas was: "Come with me, I'll set this thing straight with these men. They trust me." Barnabas would represent Saul before the apostles and shared with them the miraculous transformation that had taken place with Saul. Barnabas was indicating that he believed Saul was authentic and genuine. He had observed this transformation first-hand and was willing to recommend that the apostles and Christian community accept and make room for Saul. Additionally, they

17. Resolute

needed to relax and set aside any prejudice or fear they had embraced toward Saul.

Would there be any change as a result of Barnabas having endorsed and recommended Saul? A concluding statement by Swindoll is: "The result of Barnabas's action on behalf of Saul was - Saul was with them, moving about freely in Jerusalem, speaking out boldly in the name of the Lord. For the first time in his ministry, Saul spoke freely about Christ in Jerusalem, in the company of respected disciples—set free to be himself for the glory of God. What made the difference? Barnabas!"

When Jesus was training the twelve, there was the occasion for a lesson to be learned when He encountered the Samaritan woman at Jacob's well. This woman had been married five times and had little hope of being anything other than a woman with a negative image before others. Without using the proper name of Barnabas, Jesus was indicating that this woman was a person who needed someone who would be an encouragement in her life so that transformation would fully occur. He wanted His disciples to learn what a Barnabas is and that which a Barnabas does. Did the disciples grasp this enthusiastically? No! Were they ready, as Jews, to accept a stranger who was a despised Samaritan? No! Were the disciples any different than many, or most, Christians are today? No!

The area for self-examination is whether or not we are willing to take a stand for the one who has been or is being oppressed! The measuring also includes whether or not we are ready to stand for the isolated one. Are we ready and willing to be a Barnabas in his or her life?

Jesus said to His disciples (John 4); "Forget about secular thinking about seasons and harvests. Get focused on the spiritual potential. Look who is returning with the people of Sychar being led by this marginalized woman. They are coming to Me – Jesus!" As a result, many people embraced Jesus Christ as The Messiah. They believed, as had the woman, and their lives were eternally changed, Do you believe that this type of ministry could be part of your personal Barnabas activity? When I was a boy, a hymn that was sung contained these words of a Barnabas vision and commitment:

> Give me a passion for souls, dear Lord,
> A passion to save the lost;
> O that Thy love were by all adored,
> And welcomed at any cost.

> Though there are dangers untold and stern
> Confronting me in the way,
> Willingly still would I go, nor turn,
> But trust Thee for grace each day.
> Refrain
> Jesus, I long, I long to be winning
> Men who are lost, and constantly sinning;
> O may this hour be one of beginning
> The story of pardon to tell.

18. Frustration

When you think about your Christian walk and spiritual growth, are there moments when you wonder why your influence and success seems to be limited? If so, does that cause inner-frustration? When attempting to do a Barnabas ministry with an individual and the response is negative rather than positive, does that cause some angst (feeling of anxiety or anguish) within you? Frustration creeps in and the one to whom you are ministering has a sense of dissatisfaction, sometimes leading to depression because of unfulfilled needs or unresolved problems.

Barnabas was a unique servant of the Lord who sought to encourage and comfort others who were facing trying circumstances or were being marginalized because of past behavior and a negative reputation. Barnabas reached out to such individuals and attempted to make a positive out of a negative situation. Such is the case with Paul (a new name for a renewed man). In Acts 9:27, when the world seemed to be fearful and opposed to Saul of Tarsus, we find the purposeful phrase: "But Barnabas."

Acts 9:1-2 (NIV) begins with: "Saul was still breathing out murderous threats against the Lord's disciples. He went to the high priest and asked him for letters to the synagogues in Damascus, so that if he found any there who belonged to the Way, whether men or women, he might take them as prisoners to Jerusalem." Saul meets Jesus on the road to Damascus and is converted to the Christianity he was working to eliminate. The apostles were reluctant to receive and accept him as a brother in Christ. Not so with Barnabas. Acts 9:27 shares with us the act of Barnabas who gave his encouragement, endorsement and recommendation of Saul to the apostles. The text states: "But Barnabas took him and brought him to the apostles. He told them how Saul on his journey had seen the Lord and that the Lord had spoken to him, and how in Damascus he had preached fearlessly in the name of Jesus." Barnabas had credibility with the apostles and told them to accept Saul as "being one of us."

Following Saul's conversion, his name was soon referenced as Paul. Paul and Barnabas are close friends and confront the instruction that was causing division among the people. They were told: "Unless you are circumcised, according to the custom taught by Moses, you cannot be saved." As more and more Gentiles were being converted, it increased the fervor of the Hellenistic Jews and others to champion their cause that required circumcision on the part of all the Gentile converts.

Peter stood up before the apostles and informed them of the increasing numbers of Gentiles who believe in the Lord Jesus Christ. Then James stood up and said: "Listen to me. Simon has described to us how God first intervened to choose a people for his name from the Gentiles. The words of the prophets are in agreement." The solution offered by James for the Gentiles is:

18. Frustration

> It is my judgment...that we should not make it difficult for the Gentiles who are turning to God. Instead we should write to them, telling them to abstain from food polluted by idols, from sexual immorality, from the meat of strangled animals and from blood.

James wanted the people to give their attention to God's requirements. The Jerusalem Council listened to the wise counsel offered.

> Then the apostles and elders, with the whole church, decided to choose some of their own men and send them to Antioch with Paul and Barnabas. They chose Judas (called Barsabbas) and Silas, men who were leaders among the believers.

So far, so good. There is agreement that the mission of the Church must be enlarged. As wise and as good as the vision for church growth was a disagreement that would arise resulting in tension between Paul and Barnabas. Acts 15:38-40 describes the degree of the tension which would lead to a breach between Barnabas and Paul.

> Paul said to Barnabas: Let us go back and visit the believers in all the towns where we preached the word of the Lord and see how they are doing. Barnabas wanted to take John, also called Mark, with them, but Paul did not think it wise to take him, because he had

deserted them in Pamphylia and had not continued with them in the work.

What had John Mark done that caused him to be unacceptable for the expanding ministry? Why was Paul judgmental in his opposition toward John Mark? Had he forgotten his own old reputation about bad deeds? Even if John Mark had failed, was he not worthy to be granted a second chance? Verses 39-40 states: "They had such a sharp disagreement that they parted company. Barnabas took Mark and sailed for Cyprus but Paul chose Silas and left, commended by the believers to the grace of the Lord." Was Barnabas acting authoritatively and dictatorially as a decision maker over Paul? Had Paul relapsed to be ego-driven as he was in his former life and had he forgotten to be humble and open-minded to the alternative choice(s) of others - of a Barnabas? Was the action of Barnabas because he saw the potential for rehabilitation of John Mark for future trust and involvement in doing kingdom work? What happened to Barnabas and John Mark in their ministry effort? We don't hear or learn much more about Barnabas and only a small reference to John Mark is made by Paul near the end of his life.

Obviously, we learn much more about Paul due to his extensive writing (13 books/epistles) in the New Testament. We don't know what John Mark did in past ministry with Paul. Barnabas was no lesser than Paul in spreading the gospel but very little is mentioned about him. Why? Was Paul an

18. Frustration

egoist and authoritarian in whatever he did? He will go on to emphasize his embraced title: "Paul an apostle." He rarely inserted an alternative word "Paul a servant."

Did Barnabas have successful input in the mentoring and restoration of John Mark? Some commentators suggest Mark wrote the Gospel of Mark on behalf of Peter who would have dictated his remembrances about and experiences during the ministry of Jesus. Later on, near the end of his life, Paul is found reminiscing and thinking about those who would faithfully fill the gap after his departure. We find him saying (Second Timothy 4:11 – NLT), "Only Luke is with me. Bring Mark with you when you come, for he will be helpful to me in my ministry." Could this be an admission that perhaps he erred in his earlier thought and decision about John Mark? Was he, in effect, being complementary toward Barnabas – "I knew he would faithfully encourage John Mark so he could be useful in this ministry once again?" Would Paul have gained some humility during his long journeys and difficult experiences and was now toning down some of his prideful rhetoric and actions? Some of these questions are unanswerable. What we do know Biblically is that God wants his servants to be humble in all things and at all times as they serve Him.

In December 2017, the Huffington Post printed an article about being humble in philosophy and religion. Some of the points made included: "People who practice humility tend to reflect inward, but when it comes to where they focus their energy, it's all about other people. They have a real interest in others and their contributions to the world…Humble people are more likely than prideful people to help out a friend…Humble people show a more charitable and generous nature toward other people. With humility…you're more capable of waiting for the peaks of your life to come and you're grateful when they do…"

As one thinks about Barnabas, it is not just the prominence of his encouragement but also his humility and servant's heart that are obvious. Perhaps that should cause all of us to offer as the prayer of our heart and life the following words/prayer - - -

> Make me a servant Humble and meek
> Lord let me lift up those who are weak.
> And may the prayers of my heart always be
> Make me a servant, Make me a servant,
> Make me a servant today.

19 Eagerness

There are times when one can feel overwhelmed by the pressures of life and hostile experiences. In times past, I have been very grateful for the words in Isaiah 40:28-31 (NLT),

> The LORD is the everlasting God...He never grows weak or weary...He gives power to the weak and strength to the powerless. Even youths will become weak and tired, and young men will fall in exhaustion.

These verses express the occasion of a person falling under the weight of exhaustion. A hymn written in 1862 asks the question: "Art thou weary, art thou languid, Art thou sore distressed?" The answer is affirmative when the weight and disappointments of ministry and Christian lifestyle bring one close to anxiety. The seventh stanza of the hymn has one final question and response:

> Finding, following, keeping, struggling,
> Is He sure to bless?
> Saints, apostles, prophets, martyrs,
> Answer, Yes!"

How can this be when the pressures are so much greater than one's human capabilities? Isaiah 40:31 (NLT) indicates:

"Those who trust in the LORD will find new strength…will soar high on wings like eagles…will run and not grow weary…will walk and not faint."

During the forward motion of church expansion and growth, Paul recorded in Second Corinthians 4:8-11 (NLT):

> We are pressed on every side by troubles, but we are not crushed. We are perplexed, but not driven to despair. We are hunted down, but never abandoned by God. We get knocked down, but we are not destroyed. Through suffering, our bodies continue to share in the death of Jesus so that the life of Jesus may also be seen in our bodies. Yes, we live under constant danger of death because we serve Jesus, so that the life of Jesus will be evident in our dying bodies.

On June 21, 2020 in a devotional, Charles Swindoll raises an important question and thought:

> Have you ever felt the sting…of rejection? Have you ever had such a bad track record that people didn't want to associate with you or welcome you into their fellowship?…People are rejected because of their past. The load of baggage they drag behind them as they enter the Christian life keeps them from enjoying what should be instant acceptance. The rejection at times is unbearable…Thankfully, in the midst of those times, God faithfully provides lesser-known individuals who

19 Eagerness

come alongside and say: Hey, I'm on your team. Let me walk through this with you. Who would do this? His name is Barnabas, the encourager.

Barnabas was a person who served as an example of Peter's instruction to the persecuted church. He epitomizes First Peter 1:13-14 (NLT),

> So prepare your minds for action and exercise self-control. Put all your hope in the gracious salvation that will come to you when Jesus Christ is revealed to the world. So you must live as God's obedient child.

This describes who, how and what Barnabas was and did as a servant of the Lord. He was unafraid and uninhibited when it came to doing any task. He did not shrink back from the difficult challenge. It mattered little to him if everyone was opposed to a Saul of Tarsus. The Lord had chosen Saul and Barnabas befriended him so he could be the most effective servant possible. Was it risky? Yes! What is his focus and fearless ministry? To face any situation in the strength of the Lord. He was ready to do the will of God despite any personal cost or rejection.

In a strange way, many can cope better when the challenges are greater and the situations are more difficult. A persistent problem is one of most trying moments experienced in life. Words of criticism can shatter one and remove the wind in the sails of one's life. Not only is it the words that are directed at one but also the body language or a look of disapproval that can cause one to lose enthusiasm for the task one wanted to do. These actions cause one to succumb to peer pressure and group approval. Being accepted by dear friends and/or church members becomes a priority. Swindoll wrote:

Do you know someone who has been kicked in the teeth because he has a bad track record? Someone who can't get a hearing, yet she/he turned her/his life around and nobody wants to believe it?

We can sometimes be impervious to the feelings and struggles of others. We can become preoccupied with self-interests and neglect the one who wants and needs to be accepted and encouraged. When that happens, Swindoll goes on to write:

> I urge you to step up like Barnabas did for Saul. Look for those individuals who need a second chance - a large dose of grace to help them start over in the Christian life. Everybody needs a Barnabas at one time or another.

When Jesus addressed the Pharisees of His day, he pointed out that their lifestyle had a negative effect upon others. In Matthew 12:36-37, Jesus said: "I tell you this, you must give an account on judgment day for every idle word you speak. The words you say will either acquit you or condemn you." In keeping with this statement of Jesus, a Sunday School chorus children sing include the words: "Be careful little mouth what

19 Eagerness

you say...The Father up above looks down in tender love, So be careful little mouth what you say." The Psalmist emphasized in his personal prayer (Psalm 19:14 – NLT): "May the words of my mouth and the meditation of my heart be pleasing to you, O LORD, my rock and my redeemer."

The lessons and guidelines King Lemuel learned from his mother are recorded in Proverbs 31:8-9. He studies these truths , and others, as they address behaviors for life. His mother taught him: "Speak up for those who cannot speak for themselves, for the rights of all who are destitute. Speak up and judge fairly; defend the rights of the poor and needy." These proverbs represent the beginning point for all who would walk uprightly before the Lord. Do you know anyone who cannot speak up for themselves? What about those heading toward abortion? What about the orphan or the one who has been abandoned? Do you know anyone who is destitute? Can you seek out one who is destitute? Do you know some who are poor and needy? What will you do to alleviate their poverty and hunger? Don't excuse yourself from the Barnabas ministry opportunity that is present in the area where you live. Remember the words of Jesus Christ to the sheep, Matthew 25:34-36 (NKJV): "The King will say to those on His right hand:

> Come, you blessed of My Father, inherit the kingdom prepared for you from the foundation of the world: for I was hungry and you gave Me food; I was thirsty and you gave Me drink; I was a stranger and you took Me

in; I was naked and you clothed Me; I was sick and you visited Me; I was in prison and you came to Me.

What will Jesus say to you in the day when He separates the sheep from the goats? Which group will you be in - the sheep or the goats? If you are uncertain, what should you begin to do immediately? Can you be God's Barnabas in today's eroding and decaying world? Will needy, deprived and neglected people be glad that you passed their way and cared for them?

> Lord, I make a full surrender,
> All I yield to Thee;
> For Thy love, so great and tender,
> Asks the gift of me.

20. Equipped

When Jesus began to select disciples to follow Him, He first called two fishermen, Peter and Andrew. His words were both startling and compelling. These were men who knew about fishing for fish. They heard one statement from Jesus Christ as He passed where they were fishing - Matthew 4:19 (NLT), "Come, follow me, and I will show you how to fish for people!" There were two possible responses: (1) Ignore the words of this unknown person, or (2) Respond affirmatively to His invitation. Their response was: "They left their nets at once (immediately) and followed him" (Matthew 4:20).

How does this apply to the contemporary church and Biblical Christian in the twenty-first century? There is a similar compelling invitation stated by Jesus Christ. Matthew 11:28-30 (NASB),

> Come to Me, all who are weary and heavy-laden, and I will give you rest. Take My yoke upon you and learn from Me, for I am gentle and humble in heart, and you will find rest for your souls. For My yoke is easy and My burden is light.

There is an old Hymn based upon these verses in Matthew that include the lyric:

> Come, ye that seem to toil in vain,

James Perry

> Beneath a load of grief and pain;
> Come, cast on Me your every care,
> The yoke of blessed fellowship wear…
> And I will give you rest.

The compelling words are for one to "come" to Jesus and "learn" all about who He is and what He wants one to make known about Him. The idea in these verses is also indicates that the call of Jesus Christ to "Come" was not limited to twelve men during the days that Jesus ministered on the earth but to all who would respond to His call throughout all generations. What are some of the things Jesus wants His followers to learn from and about Him? He states three areas in Matthew 11.

> First, learn about the meekness of Him.
> Second, learn about His lowliness (humility).
> Third, learn about resting in the Lord.

Paul summarized these thoughts when he wrote in Philippians 2:5-8 (ESV),

> Have this mind among yourselves, which is yours in Christ Jesus, who though he was in the form of God, did not count equality with God a thing to be grasped, but emptied himself, by taking the form of a servant, being born in the likeness of men. And being found in

20. Equipped

human form, he humbled himself by becoming obedient to the point of death, even death on a cross.

These verses in the MSG are paraphrased:

> Think of yourselves the way Christ Jesus thought of himself. He had equal status with God but didn't think so much of himself that he had to cling to the advantages of that status no matter what. Not at all. When the time came, he set aside the privileges of deity and took on the status of a slave...Having become human, he stayed human. It was an incredibly humbling process. He didn't claim special privileges. Instead, he lived a selfless, obedient life and then died a selfless, obedient death - and the worst kind of death at that - a crucifixion.

Jesus continues to want His followers to learn this lifestyle and to exhibit these spiritual traits. There are many lessons one should learn about the Lord and Master. Some of them are summarized in Scripture by the use of the "let us" phrase. If one is to effectively serve and function as a contemporary Barnabas, what is the encouragement that is to be shared? The Book of Hebrews contains several of the "let us" phrases. One grouping is found in Hebrews 10:22-25 (ESV):

> Let us draw near with a true heart in full assurance of faith, with our hearts sprinkled clean from an evil conscience and our bodies washed with pure water.
> Let us hold fast the confession of our hope without wavering, for he who promised is faithful.
> Let us consider how to stir up one another to love and good works. (Let us) not neglect to meet together, as is the habit of some, (Let us) encourage one another, and all the more as you see the Day drawing near.

Hebrews 12:1-2 (ESV) adds:

> Let us also lay aside every weight, and sin which clings so closely, and Let us run with endurance the race that is set before us, (Let us keep on) looking to Jesus, the founder and perfecter of our faith, who for the joy that was set before him endured the cross, despising the shame, and is seated at the right hand of the throne of God.

These same verses in The Message boldly assert:

> Strip down, start running and never quit! No extra spiritual fat, no parasitic sins.
> Keep your eyes on Jesus, who both began and finished this race we're in.
> Study how he did it. Because he never lost sight of where he was headed - that exhilarating finish in and

20. Equipped

with God - he could put up with anything along the way: Cross, shame, whatever. And now he's there, in the place of honor, right alongside God.

When you find yourselves flagging in your faith, go over that story again, item by item, that long litany of hostility he plowed through. That will/should shoot adrenaline into your souls!

How do people know you? Do they see in you a similarity to Barnabas? Do they know you as an encourager and one who takes a stand for the marginalized? Do they look forward to being alongside of you in their spiritual journey? I have a friend who sometimes encounters the issue of what his name conveys to those who do not know him personally. His name is Dr. D. Clair Davis, who ministered several years teaching Church History in a well-known Seminary. His former students know who he is, but the mass-mailers do not. He often receives mail addressed to either "Mrs." Or "Ms." Clair Davis. Recently, he wrote a Blog entitled Your Personal Jesus. He wrote:

> My name could be either a woman's or a man's. It used to cheer me up a lot that Claire Chennault was head of the Flying Tigers. Mail is the worst. It used to come to Mrs. It's some improvement that now it comes to Ms. But while those letters keep telling me where I live and what my name is, when they keep on calling me 'Ms.' they lose their punch. It's hard to believe that

they know me as well as their computer lets on. Getting my name right is crucial. Is it that way with you?

Do you think there's more to you than what the computer says? Do you amount to more than your credit rating and the number of points in your driving record? Do you think Freud must be wrong, that there's more to you than childhood sexuality? Do you think Marx must be wrong, that you're more than cannon fodder in the class struggle? Do you keep thinking you're a significant person?

Then you're agreeing with the Lord. He takes you totally seriously as an individual. He treats you as a person, not as a result. He holds you responsible for what you do and for what you become.

Think about the last sentence above: "The Lord holds you responsible for what you do and for what you become." That brings us back to your personal Barnabas Quest. How closely are you becoming like a Barnabas among the people with whom you mingle and those who you pass by? Do they see and know you as one whom they are pleased and overjoyed to see? Or, do they see you as a pretender and insincere in your expressed words?

There is a brief worship chorus that expresses an apt pursuit and prayer for the Biblical Christian. This was the goal and mission for Barnabas - it can and should be a major spiritual commitment for you as well.

20. Equipped

To be like Jesus, to be like Jesus
All I ask to be like Him;
All through life's journey From earth to glory
All I ask to be like Him.

To be like Jesus, to be like Jesus
All I ask to be like Him;
Not in a measure but in its fullness
All I ask to be like Him.

21. Teachability

When Jesus called the twelve disciples to follow Him, He stated: "I will make you…" Some of them knew how to fish for fish, but Jesus would teach them how to fish for people. Those with other skills would soon learn the practical usefulness for their gifts as they use those skills for a completely different objective – reaching out to people with the Gospel. Later on, when the appeal to follow Jesus was extended in a much broader way, Jesus included: "Come! Learn about Me…" To both calls and urgings, the emphasis was on learning that which Jesus would be teaching them. This is also foundational for anyone who desires to be a Barnabas to others. Barnabas had to be teachable. Those whose lives he touched would know by his care and manner that he had embraced who Jesus is and had learned great foundational truths about Him.

Teachability is not always an easy process. It is a discipline to increase one's knowledge and to change one's ensuing behavior. For the disciples and all who followed Jesus, it was transformative. The process included old things and ways being left behind and all things being taught by Jesus being emulated and utilized (Second Corinthians 5:17). It was learning new methods and new behaviors. It was a change in focus and commitment. This process reminds me of a simple worship song that expresses some of this transformative learning:

James Perry

> Sad broken hearted, at an altar I knelt.
> I found peace that was so serene.
> And all that He asks is a child-like trust
> And a heart that is learning to lean.

Refrain:

> Learning to lean, Learning to lean,
> I'm learning to lean on Jesus.
> Finding more power than I've ever dreamed
> I'm learning to lean on Jesus.

> There's a glorious victory, each day now for me
> I've found peace so serene.
> He helps me with each task, If I'll only ask,
> Every day now I'm learning to lean.

In His day, one of the titles by which Jesus was known was Rabbi or Teacher. One of the references that identifies who Jesus is occurs in John 3:1-2 (NIV) when a Pharisee, Nicodemus, came to Jesus by night and said to Him: "Rabbi, we know that you are a teacher who has come from God." This assertion of Nicodemus was correct but there was more to his time in the presence of Jesus. Nicodemus had questions that needed answers. Did Nicodemus believe the answers given by Jesus and then become one of his followers? John 3 doesn't grant us that insight. We can deduce it from a different passage that Nicodemus may have been more than curious

21. Teachability

about Jesus and His teaching. We know he was present at the crucifixion of Jesus when most of the disciples of Jesus had hidden in fear. In John 19:28-40 (NIV) we read:

> Joseph of Arimathea asked Pilate for the body of Jesus. Now Joseph was a disciple of Jesus, but secretly because he feared the Jewish leaders. With Pilate's permission, he came and took the body away. He was accompanied by Nicodemus, the man who earlier had visited Jesus at night. Nicodemus brought a mixture of myrrh and aloes, about seventy-five pounds. Taking Jesus' body, the two of them wrapped it, with the spices, in strips of linen. This was in accordance with Jewish burial customs.

While this does not prove his belief in Jesus Christ or his commitment to follow Him, he was present at a very crucial and critical moment as Christ's physical life was slowly ebbing out of Him. It appears that those things the Rabbi, (Teacher), Jesus instructed and modelled made an impression on Nicodemus as well as on others. Addressing Jesus as Rabbi (Teacher) is one thing - being committed to Him and following Him is another. Teachability is the aim of Jesus for the lives of those He called to follow Him.

One of the things Jesus made known to His disciples included His purpose. John 10:10 (ESV), "I have come that they may have life and have it more abundantly." The NLT paraphrase is: "My purpose is to give them a rich and satisfying life." If they were to survive during this transition and transformation in their lives, they had to learn to trust Jesus Christ implicitly. This is no less of a requirement within the twenty-first century call to follow Jesus. Part of having abundant life in Jesus Christ is to have an unshakable and non-equivocal faith. If you carefully read the Gospels, the occasional phrases spoken to the disciples addressed their "little faith" or "no faith" in either Jesus Christ or their realized experiences.

The content of who Jesus Christ is and why He came to this earth is summarized in Luke 19:10 (ESV), Jesus had a meeting with Zacchaeus. He said to Zacchaeus and to those who grumbled about the time Jesus spent with him, there is something you need to learn about me and my methods: "The Son of Man came to seek and to save the lost."

As Jesus was revealing Himself in His teaching and miracles, there was another important lesson He wanted His disciples to observe and learn. It occurs in John 13:12-20 (ESV) before the Feast of the Passover. Jesus gathered with His disciples for supper. Beforehand, Jesus assumed the role of a servant by His act of washing the feet of the disciples. It was another learning moment, especially when He asked them a question (Verse 12): "Do you understand what I have done to you?" Rather than entering into a discussion or debate with the disciples, Jesus proceeds to give them the response they must learn and apply (Verse 15): "I have given you an example, that you should also do just as I have done to you."

21. Teachability

What does this response and application have to do with their calling? What important lesson does He want them to learn? The answer is in Verse 16: "I say to you, a servant is not greater than his master, nor is a messenger greater than the one who sent him." If the disciples are going to be effective in ministry, their Master, Jesus Christ, must not only be declared by them but also seen living in and through them. This is equally true for each one of us whether engaged in a Barnabas-type ministry of encouragement or as one who is applying the spiritual gifts given to them by the Lord.

The prayer and song flowing from the heart of all disciples everywhere should be the words written by Charles Gabriel in 1906:

> More like the Master I would ever be,
> More of His meekness, more humility;
> More zeal to labor, more courage to be true,
> More consecration for work He bids me do.

Refrain:

> Take Thou my heart, I would be Thine alone;
> Take Thou my heart, and make it all Thine own.
> Amen!

22. Shadows

On June 26, 2020, Chuck Swindoll published a devotional – Out of the Shadows. In it, he wrote:

> Some of you who read these words today could use a little extra hope, especially if you find yourself in a waiting mode. You were once engaged in the action, doing top-priority work on the front lines. No longer. All that has changed. Now, for some reason, you're on the shelf. It's tough to stay encouraged perched on a shelf. Your mind starts playing tricks on you. Though you are well-educated, experienced, and fairly gifted in your particular field, you are now waiting. You're wondering, and maybe you're getting worried, that this waiting period might be permanent. You can't see any light at the end of the tunnel. It just doesn't seem fair. After all, you've trained hard, you've jumped through hoops, and you've even made the necessary sacrifices. Discouragement crouches at the door, ready to pounce on any thought or hope, so you sit wondering why God has chosen to pass you by.

If you've never been there – Wait! Sooner or later you may be and wondering: "What did I do to deserve this?" Swindoll includes a quote from James Stalker: "Waiting is a common instrument of providential discipline for those to whom exceptional work has been appointed." Swindoll encourages one to re-read that statement slowly and let it sink into one's spiritual mindset. Being in the shadows of God's will and purpose is not an easy road to travel. Inwardly, you can find yourself eager to get back into action but there seems to be no place available. I mused with my close companion whether or not my horizon was too limited and narrow. Maybe I should broaden it and move into new situations – a new direction. Our musing conjured the idea that perhaps the other side to this eagerness is that the Lord is trying to communicate: "It's best that you come apart to rest and regain your perspective and priorities before you just come apart!"

This idea echoes the words of the motivational speaker, Dallas Willard, who often suggested: "If you don't come apart for a while, you will come apart after a while." He based this on the words of Jesus Christ to His disciples after a very busy period in their lives. In Mark 6:30-31 (NLT) we read that: "The apostles returned to Jesus from their ministry tour and told him all they had done and taught. Then Jesus said: Let's go off by ourselves to a quiet place and rest awhile. He said this because there were so many people coming and going that Jesus and his apostles didn't even have time to eat." In the MSG: "Jesus said: Come off by yourselves; let's take a break and get a little rest." And, in the NKJV: "Jesus said to them: Come aside by yourselves to a deserted place and rest a while."

While thinking on these words shared by Dallas Willard, another Motivational Speaker, Ginger Ciminello, asked herself

22. Shadows

questions about her own priorities, questions each of us might do well to ask of ourselves:

> Where do I notice God at work in my life?
> Who or what am I worshipping with my life?
> How and where can I simplify?
> How can I further let self-discovery be the by-product of God-discovery?

In the June 27, 2020 Devotional, Chuck Swindoll wrote about God's waiting room. Some of what he suggested and shared was:

> Your time of God-ordained waiting will never be all that significant in other people's minds. All they may know is that you dropped out of sight. You're gone from the scene. It may begin with a bankruptcy. It may start with a horrible experience you go through, such as a tragic accident or a devastating illness. You may endure the pain of a torn reputation caused by someone who didn't tell the truth. All that devastation has a way of breaking you. The Lord uses the disappointment to lead you to His waiting room. There He begins to work deep within your soul until you can honestly confess: When I am weak, He is strong (Second Corinthians 12:9-10). When that happens, you will be ready to come out of the shadows.

Can that take place in the life of a Barnabas? Yes! Is it easier for him or more difficult? More difficult! Is Barnabas content and relaxed in God's waiting room? No! Will there be a time, place or moment when God will place Barnabas where He wants him to minister for Him? Yes! What can a Barnabas do while it seems to be endless waiting? Maybe he needs to remind himself of Psalm 37:1-7 where David shared some of his thoughts and principles for his walk with the Lord:

> Don't worry or envy
> Trust in the Lord and do good.
> Take delight in the Lord, and he will give you your heart's desires.
> Commit everything you do to the Lord.
> Trust him, and he will help you.
> Be still (quiet, relaxed, resting) in the presence of the Lord, and
> Wait patiently (don't be anxious or in a rush) for him to act.
> Don't worry about evil people
> Don't fret about their wicked schemes.

IF ONLY, these principles were actually mine. IF ONLY, I knew why God's waiting room was a necessary place for me. IF ONLY...

Why does God place any of us in His waiting room for a period of time? Why is the temporary period of "shadows" basic for my learning what God wants me to know about Him?

22. Shadows

A Barnabas friend, Steve Sellers, has found great comfort from the words in Psalm 91. He has shared this with me frequently. Psalm 91:1 (NLT) states this meaningful truth: "Those who live in the shelter of the Most High will find rest in the shadow of the Almighty." The shadow of Almighty God is where I can rest in Him and learn more about His will for me.

In 1901, Irvin H. Mack wrote the words to a hymn entitled Light Beyond The Shadows. It's one of the hymns that, regrettably, is almost never sung. It is a hymn of hope and encouragement. The lyrics remind us:

> When the troubles gather And the billows roll,
> Dark the way before you, Cares oppress the soul,
> There is blessed sunshine Just beyond your view;
> Often but a trial You are going through.
>
> Though you cannot fathom Why you're called to bear
> All the heavy burdens That you cannot share,
> Keep the cross before you In the darkest day;
> Put your trust in Jesus All along the way.
>
> Go with faith to conquer Trials that appear;
> Know that Christ your Savior With His help is near;
> Never give up the battle, Hard though it may be,
> For your Lord has promised You the victory.

Refrain:

James Perry

See the sunlight, Shining bright and clear;
Blessed sunlight Drives away all fear;
Look above you, Clouds will disappear;
Put your trust in Jesus, He is ever near.

In 1868, Horatio R, Palmer wrote the hymn, Yield Not To Temptation. The refrain reminds each of us who may be with us in God's waiting room and the temporary shadows:

Ask the Savior to help you,
Comfort, strengthen, and keep you;
He is willing to aid you,
He will carry you through.
Amen!

23. Breakthrough

When one is in the shadows, it can be a safe and enduring place. It is the place where one should remember who is present there and how He is protective of His own. The servant and child of the Lord must always remember positionally where they are: (Psalm 91:1-NLT), "Those who live in the shelter of the Most High will find rest in the shadow of the Almighty." Why would anyone complain about being in the shadow of the Almighty? There is a danger when one feels forgotten, unwanted, unneeded, and no longer useful. It's hard to sit in the shadows when it seems that those who have lesser skill sets are highly involved in ministry rather than the one with a Barnabas heart who is eager to be engaged in active and ongoing ministry but is not. It produces a restlessness and impatience with what appears to be endless waiting.

Is that apparent endless waiting without an eternal purpose? Could that time in God's waiting room equate with being in God's workshop as He hones and shapes one for more effective ministry? In June 2020, Chuck Swindoll shared four principles for why one should be trusting God in the shadows. In the time when God brings us into the shadow of His wings (His waiting room), what should one keep in mind? Swindoll said:

> When God prepares us for effective ministry, He includes what we would rather omit—a period of waiting. That cultivates patience.
>
> When God makes us wait, hiding us in His shadow, He shows us we're not indispensable. That makes us humble.
>
> While God hides us away, He reveals new dimensions of Himself and new insights regarding ministry. That makes us deep.
>
> When God finally chooses to use us, it comes at a time least expected, when we feel the least qualified. That makes us effective.

One of the potential dangers in waiting is that it can lead one into thinking that God has put him/her on a shelf. It is at such a time that the enemy of one's spiritual life will try to find an entrance and plant seeds that one is no longer central or useful to the Lord, that one's shelf-life has expired. The meaning of shelf-life is twofold. (1) It is a period of time when a stored commodity remains usable, effective or suitable; service/serviceable life. Or, (2) An expiration date when a commodity is no longer safe for use. Paul had reached that point when he decided that John Mark was no longer effective or useful. He did not suggest that John Mark should be put on the shelf for a limited time to learn the principles of God for more effective ministry. Paul's judgment was that John Mark's shelf-life had expired.

23. Breakthrough

Barnabas had a different opinion and that's when a breach occurred between Barnabas and Paul. Sadly, we find these judgments and assessments about a person's effectiveness too often. People are marginalized by those who believe they have the authority to make that judgment and reach their decision. This is one reason it is so vital and needful for there to be a Barnabas who reaches out to one who may be walking under a shadow. Barnabas will reach remind the judged person about the shadow of the Almighty and His protective wings under which the marginalized one can find care, healing and encouragement. It is a place where spiritual break-throughs will take place and where one can become unshackled. It is a curiosity to wonder about the thoughts of Charles Wesley in 1739 when he wrote: And Can It Be? The words in the fourth stanza are:

> Long my imprisoned spirit lay,
> Fast bound in sin and nature's night;
> Thine eye diffused a quickening ray—
> I woke, the dungeon flamed with light;
> My chains fell off, my heart was free,
> I rose, went forth, and followed Thee.

Was this is an indication of one becoming unshackled by the divine power of God? Was Charles Wesley sharing a personal testimony and experience? Or, was he sharing a general Biblical truth about the amazing grace and love of an amazing God? It could be any or all of the above. The point is that a break-through can and will take place in God's waiting room. One will be unshackled and set free. It is in that waiting room that one will be reminded of John 8:36 (NASB), "If the Son makes you free, you will be free indeed." Free indeed – a break-through; one being divinely unshackled.

Over the years, I have been impressed with the long-standing ministry of the Pacific Garden Mission in Chicago, Illinois. Founded in 1877, it is one of the oldest shelters and rescue missions in the nation. Interestingly, in past years, two men who resided in the shelter for a period of time went on to be evangelists – Billy Sunday and Mel Trotter. In 1950, a radio program began to be broadcast – Unshackled – a dramatic program continuing to this day which shares the conversions of various ones who found their way into the Mission. In each biographical sketch, the summary is that another one has become – Unshackled.

In past months, I have often thought about the story of one who had been an effective and highly capable pastor and a husband who had fathered four children who slipped and fell from his faith . Despite the efforts of some, he was defrocked, divorced, and began to drift further into dangerous indulgences. His actions lead to his being arrested for making pornography available to underaged young people and facilitating prostitution. There were thirteen felony counts from just a partial investigation of his activities. He lost his teaching position and kept on drifting. With a trial looming, he drove out of town and made the tragic choice to commit suicide. It would be too easy to judge such a one harshly rather

23. Breakthrough

than pause and think that "but for the grace of God go I." The origin of the quote is attributed to John Bradford and was prompted by a group of criminals being led to their executions.

IF ONLY a Barnabas had been able to mentor the former Pastor and those being led to their execution, the outcome would have had a more positive conclusion. IF ONLY, I would remember the position that is mine in Jesus Christ – secure in His hand (John 10) and under the shadow of the wings of the Almighty (Psalm 91).

Years ago, I had the privilege of travelling with groups that were a type of gospel team. One who travelled frequently with the group was a young and gifted violinist. A selection that he would often play was: Overshadowed. Someone would usually follow by sharing the meaningful lyric with those in attendance. The words of that Hymn address the desired break-through, being unshackled and having a usable shelf-life for the Lord.

OVERSHADOWED

How desolate my life would be,
How dark and dreary my nights and days,
If Jesus' face I did not see,
To brighten all earth's weary ways.

CHORUS:

James Perry

I'm overshadowed by His mighty love;
Love eternal, changeless pure.
Overshadowed by His mighty love;
Rest is mine, serene, secure.
He died to ransom me from sin,
He lives to keep me day by day,
I'm overshadowed by his mighty love,
Love that brightens all my way.

With burdened heart I wandered long,
By grief and unbelief distressed;
But now I sing faith's happy song,
In Christ my Savior I am blest.

Now judgment fears no more alarm,
I dread no death, nor Satan's power;
The world for me has lost its charm,
God's grace sustains me every hour.

Amen.

24. Influencers

The years of one's life pass all too quickly. Sometimes, it is with the absence of those who had influence in shaping one's life. One of my earliest memories is when I was seven years of age following the death of my father. Soon after his death, we moved from an area in Queens, New York where the neighborhood and public school was clean and functioned with high standards. My mother moved us to the Bushwick/Greenpoint section of Brooklyn, New York. To me, it was a grungy area. The neighborhood and public school were almost antithetical to where we had previously lived and were being educated. I was the youngest of three children and never had the sense of fitting into either the neighborhood or school.

Despite my personal feelings, I had a teacher who I failed to fully appreciate at that time. The school classroom had double classes. I entered into Grade 3A that also contained Grade 3B. I felt lost and alone in this new situation. However, this teacher, Mrs. Halloran, looked with kindness on me. She essentially was a secular Barnabas. She encouraged me and did her best to assist me. In later years, I often wished there was a way for me to contact her and let her know her efforts were not in vain. She saw something in me that I was incapable of seeing or sensing in myself. Whether she was a Biblical Christian or not, I do not know. All I know is that she displayed a Barnabas encouragement to one who was losing his way. She cared when few others even noticed I was there.

There would be long gaps before anyone came alongside of me as a Barnabas. When I was transitioning into my teenage years, I began to feel as though the small church I had been attending viewed me only as a number – not as a person. It was easy to withdraw from that group and not go to church anywhere. I tried visiting other places but my level of interest was more quenched than not. After a few weeks, a man (who became a life-long friend) from the little church came looking for me. I have no idea how long he looked. He suddenly appeared one Sunday as I was headed to an area movie theater. I had fifteen cents and would be able to spend an afternoon watching two feature films, a newsreel and cartoons. However, there was a kind but forceful Herbie who sought me out and came to take me back to church. He had a family of his own but he looked kindly on this fatherless young person who was sliding down a road of uncertainty.

Herbie was a very unlikely Barnabas candidate. He had never finished high school and his grammatical usage was not always correct. He worked for the city in the Department of Sanitation and was part of their Drum and Bugle Corp for city sponsored parades (which were often). I do not recall what he said but he was determined that I needed to come with him and get back into church. He was successful in his effort and was more than proud when I entered Bible College and began to prepare for ministry. My first pastorate was within driving distance of where he lived and he surprised me when he came

24. Influencers

with his family to attend a church service. He continued to be proud of and encouraging for his Jimmy – one of the jewels in his heavenly crown.

Being a Church Pastor is not always the easiest occupation for finding acceptance and being allowed to fit in with the group. After reading a special edition of By Faith Magazine – June 2020, my attention was drawn to an article: Grieving the Loss of My Spiritual Father. It is more of a Eulogy for a special person in the author's life but it is also descriptive of a Barnabas in the life of one who benefitted from his effort. The article's author writes about his mentor and friend, Timothy, who died due to complications from Covid-19 (Corona Virus). The author of the article shared:

> I grieve the loss of my brother with whom I've shared friendship for many good years. Through trials and troubles, fears and failures, successes and setbacks, Tim was present to cheer, guide, and challenge. Years ago, he pledged and promised his love. With diligence, he kept this vow. He was steadfast, wise, faithful, and true. I grieve that I'll not hear his commanding voice greet me by phone. Each call began: "This is the servant of the servant of the Lord." It was an unalloyed pleasure to share in conversation with him throughout each week. The Psalms were constant companions in our conversations. I'll miss his laughter and his stories, his wisdom and his wit. These were the gifts of friendship he shared.

This testimonial reminded me that there are times when a Barnabas ministry can involve more than one person. In different churches where I was privileged to serve, there were men whose lives intersected with mine as they encouraged and assisted. Men like Floyd, Cleon, Ewald, Dave, John, Frank (and several others) who entered my life at the right time to pray with and for me, to serve alongside me, and to share in the vision for ministry as the Lord revealed it to us.

Frank was an interesting person. He was a widower who longed for his heavenly home. Occasionally and without announcement, he would come to my office to see if I had time to pray with him. Frank was a human encyclopedia of Biblical references. There were times when I mentioned I was looking for a verse that included - - but before I could finish, he quoted not just the verse but the context in which it appeared. As he neared the end of his prayer, Frank would include: "Lord, keep Jim from showing either fear or favor toward man." I suspect he had in mind the words of Deuteronomy 1:16-17 (NLT),

> Moses instructed the judges: You must hear the cases of your fellow Israelites and the foreigners living among you. Be perfectly fair in your decisions and impartial in your judgments. Hear the cases of those who are poor as well as those who are rich. Don't be afraid of anyone's anger, for the decision you make is

24. Influencers

God's decision. Bring me any cases that are too difficult for you, and I will handle them.

There are others who could be mentioned and listed. There is one man of late who has become very special to me. In 2017, I was diagnosed with Stage 4, Non- Hodgkin's Lymphoma. While the doctor kindly said I should not think that it was fatal, it was difficult not to think that it was. Emerging soon thereafter, a man I had never met or spoken to, made contact with me on Facebook Messenger. The things he shared with me, that he had the same diagnoses but was now in his fifth year of remission, was encouraging. He prayed for me and encouraged me as a "mighty man of God." Near the beginning of 2019, in a routine examination, his Oncologist discovered a suspicious lump under his arm. It subjected him to several painful follow up visits and treatments. I saw this as a privilege to be a Barnabas for him and to encourage and uphold him before the Lord. But, before I could fully reciprocate, in late February 2020, I began to have difficulty swallowing, breathing, and then my speech became garbled so that no one could understand what I was saying. Following four Chemo treatments, there was no evidence that the Lymph nodes in my neck were being reduced. This necessitated radiation treatments.

Meanwhile, I knew Steve's journey was long and painful and I did not want to fail in being a Barnabas for and to him. However, on June 5, 2020 he wrote me:

June 5 will mark one year ago that I entered UAB in Birmingham, AL for my stem cell transplant. I praise the Lord for allowing me to go through this to mature in my faith, reach the lost and bring Him Glory!

Thank you for being a Man of Valor for me. Your prays and encouragement mean a lot. I am praying for you and your family.

Your Servant in Christ, Steve - Psalm 91

Twenty days after this note from Steve, I was informed by the Doctor that the PET Scan result indicated I was free of any trace of lymphoma anywhere in my body. On June 26, 2020, Steve wrote to those on his Facebook list of friends: "I want you to join me in praising the Lord that Brother James Perry's PET Scan was clear!!! He has been battling Non-Hodgkin's Lymphoma for the second time. Praise the Lord he is in Remission!!!!"

To whom are you a Barnabas? The Lord can use you to reach someone who needs encouragement and a spiritual nudge to trust in the Lord with all their heart. Will you do that for your Lord? Will you pray the words of the worship chorus?

> Make me a servant, humble and meek.
> Lord let me lift up those who are weak.
> And may the prayer of my heart always be:
> Make me a servant, make me a servant,
> make me a servant today.

25. Aspiration

If you've read this far, you may be inwardly thinking, I'm interested in a Barnabas Quest. What do I have to do and be if I am to accomplish becoming a Barnabas in my circles and my culture? When God made us, He did so that we would be in relationship and fellowship with Him. Similarly, He wants His people, who are called by His name, to be in relationship with people within the culture where He has placed and positioned them. The Lord has provided us with guidelines and directives regarding how this task can be done and accomplished. There are more than fifty references in the New Testament instructing us how we are to relate to people with whom we have some form of contact or fellowship. These references show us that the Lord is interested in our behavior and not just our attitudes. We can give inward and silent agreement with the Biblical instructions but that does nothing for those who need a Barnabas to come alongside them to encourage and to assist if that is warranted.

Some of the guidelines and directives utilize the "one another" or "each other" phrases in the New Testament. As a starting point, a few of them for your edification and application are:

>To Love One Another
>John 13:34-35: A new commandment I give to you, that you love one another: just as I have loved you, you

also are to love one another. By this all people will know that you are my disciples, if you have love for one another.

Honoring One Another
Romans 12:10 - Love one another with brotherly affection. Outdo one another in showing honor.

Serving One Another
Galatians 5:13 - For you were called to freedom, brothers. Only do not use your freedom as an opportunity for the flesh, but through love serve one another."

Patiently - Forbearing One Another
Ephesians 4:2 - with all humility and gentleness, with patience, bearing with one another in love,"

Stimulating One Another
Hebrews 10:24 - And let us consider how to stir up one another to love and good works,

Genuine Concern for One Another
First Peter 1:22 - Having purified your souls by your obedience to the truth for a sincere brotherly love, love one another earnestly from a pure heart.

Place for Unity and Humility

25. Aspiration

First Peter 3:8 - Finally, all of you, have unity of mind, sympathy, brotherly love, a tender heart, and a humble mind.

Foundational

Learning To Wait - First Corinthians 11:13
When you come together to eat, wait for one another.

Learning To Care - First Corinthians 12:25
That there may be no division in the body, but that the members may have the same care for one another.

Learning To Serve - Galatians 5:13
For you were called to freedom, brothers. Only do not use your freedom as an opportunity for the flesh, but through love serve one another.

Learning To Be Patient – Ephesians 4:2
Be completely humble and gentle; be patient, bearing with one another in love."

Four qualities that are needed to "bear with" one another:
Humility,
Gentleness,
Patience, and
Love.

An unnamed commentator stated:

> Our natural tendency is to be provoked by others especially when they do not share our ideas or convictions. When we cling to our desires rather than the well-being of others, unity is threatened and we are in danger of hurting others.

What are the behavioral and attitude changes that will exhibit a Barnabas heart? The guidelines and directives shift to a focus on the involvement of the Holy Spirit which triggers the behavior and attitude transformation that is needed (Ephesians 4:30-32 - NLT). Failure to heed the word of God will grieve and bring sorrow to the Holy Spirit. If transformation is to be valid in one's spiritual life, then certain behaviors must be removed and eradicated. Things such as, bitterness, wrath, anger, malice, evil speaking. Some of the behaviors that must be replaced is are found in the partial listing in verse 32: "Be kind to each other, tenderhearted, forgiving one another, just as God through Christ has forgiven you." Is there someone with whom you are angry or who have become objects of your evil speaking? If so, can you continue down that road of negativity and still have a Barnabas ministry? No!

What needs to immediately change in your life if (a) you will no longer bring grief to the Holy Spirit, and (b) you will be able to attain The Barnabas Quest in and for your life? Two things can occur when one's behavior and attitudes are in

25. Aspiration

accord with Biblical teaching and the Holy Spirit's requirement. First Thessalonians 5:11, "Encourage one another and build one another up..." Hebrews 3:13, "Exhort one another every day...that none of you may be hardened by the deceitfulness of sin." Hebrews 10:24-25, "Let us consider how to stir up one another to love and good works, not neglecting to meet together, as is the habit of some, but encouraging one another..."

Every Biblical Christian is to be involved in building up other professing or Biblical Christians. Encouragement and comfort is that for which Barnabas was gifted and known. A Barnabas will come alongside another to give aid and assistance. It means involvement at a personal level with those who have drifted or been marginalized. Do you know someone who needs encouragement today? Look around. Most likely many of those around you are hurting and need your encouragement to bring courage to their lives. What do you plan to do about it? Will you follow-through and do it?

Get a good concordance and look up the phrases "one another" and "each other" in the New Testament. If done carefully, you should find at least fifty-seven references. Look up the "let us" phrases both used and implied in Psalm 95 and the Book of Hebrews especially noting Hebrews 12:1-2.

A prayer you can sing and pray is significant. Just a few lines from the hymn, Speak, Lord, In the Stillness have come to mean a great deal to me.

Speak, Lord, in the stillness while I wait on Thee;

James Perry

hushed my heart to listen in expectancy.

Speak, O blessed Master, in this quiet hour;
let me see your face, Lord, feel your touch of power.

For the words You speak, Lord, they are life indeed;
living bread from heaven, now on my spirit feed!

All to You is yielded, I am not my own;
blissful, glad surrender, I am yours alone.

Fill me with the knowledge of your glorious will;
all your own good pleasure in your child fulfill.

Epilogue

Natural questions that one might ask are: Who can be a Barnabas? Two qualities must effervesce from a potential Barnabas: (a) genuineness, and (b) authenticity. Who should be a Barnabas and what is the primary responsibility of a Biblical Barnabas? The answer seems quite clear – a Barnabas should be an encourager. Three references one should always have in mind are:

1) Hebrews 3:13 (NIV), "But ENCOURAGE one another daily, as long as it is called 'Today,' so that none of you may be hardened by sin's deceitfulness."

J. B. Phillips has a helpful paraphrase: "You should therefore be most careful, my brothers, that there should not be in any of you that wickedness of heart which refuses to trust, and deserts the cause of the living God. HELP EACH OTHER to stand firm in the faith every day, while it is still called "today", and beware that none of you becomes deaf and blind to God through the delusive glamour of sin."

2) Romans 15:5 (NIV), "May the God who gives ENDURANCE AND ENCOURAGEMENT give you the same attitude of mind toward each other that Christ Jesus had,"

3) First Thessalonians 5:11 (NIV), "ENCOURAGE one another and build each other up, just as in fact you are doing."

Or, as the MSG says, "So speak ENCOURAGING WORDS to one another. Build up hope so you'll all be together in this, no one left out, no one left behind. I know you're already doing this; just keep on doing it."

A servant of the Lord mentioned throughout this book is my Barnabas, Steve Sellers. For more than three years, he has regularly written me, prayed for me, and encouraged me. After the report that there was no longer any evidence of lymphoma in my body, I wrote Steve a note. One of the things I shared with him was: "I do wonder IF or WHEN the Lord will allow me to preach His Word again. So far, all the doors and opportunities have evaporated. I may have to become a Baptist to find a place to minister??!!" Steve replied in a jocular way: "Brother eat chicken 3x in a row and you will be Baptist…Praying for the doors to open for you to preach…You are a Mighty Man of God."

A godly woman shared the following quote in her post on July 01, 2020 - Elizabeth Elliot wrote: Today is mine. Tomorrow is none of my business. If I peer anxiously into the fog of the future, I will strain my spiritual eyes so that I will not see clearly what is required of me now.

With this in mind, there are very direct words about one's self-examination, especially as it pertains to being a Barnabas within the contemporary church and culture. Take note of James 1:22-25 (NLT):

Epilogue

> Don't just listen to God's word. You must do what it says. Otherwise, you are only fooling yourselves. If you listen to the word and don't obey, it is like glancing at your face in a mirror. You see yourself, walk away, and forget what you look like. But if you look carefully into the perfect law that sets you free, and if you do what it says and don't forget what you heard, then God will bless you for doing it.

Have you taken a long, in-depth study of yourself in the mirror of God's Word? What did you see? What do you think God is seeing and knowing? Does your view and God's view align in terms of you and your priorities? Is there a discrepancy? If so, why? What will you do about it?

Another truth to remember is in John 8:31-32, 36 (NLT):

> Jesus said to the people who believed in him: You are truly my disciples if you remain faithful to my teachings. And you will know the truth, and the truth will set you free. So if the Son sets you free, you are truly free (free indeed).

Being "free indeed" is not a license to pursue one's self-interests and pleasures. "Free indeed" addresses the terms of one's salvation and hope of eternity. It is the underlying reason as to why one engages in a Barnabas ministry and the truth that is to be conveyed to the one who needs encouragement, hope and a renewed focus on Jesus Christ (Hebrews 12:2). There is a myriad of people who are marginalized, feeling unwanted and unneeded, without hope, needing to be assisted and helped. This is the opportunity for one with the Barnabas calling and commitment – stepping into the gap and endeavoring to make a difference in an individual's life and focus.

Early in 1900, A. B. Simpson wrote a poem (hymn) about the trial, suffering and death of Jesus Christ. Some of the descriptive phrases about Jesus in the hymn are:

> Jesus is standing in Pilate's hall,
> Friendless, forsaken, betrayed by all…
> Will you, like Peter, your Lord deny?

Refrain:
> What will you do with Jesus?
> Neutral you cannot be;
> Someday your heart will be asking,
> What will He do with me?

If you are ready to become a Barnabas to this culture and generation, A. B. Simpson wrote that which should be the prayer of your heart and the commitment to The Lord that you make – now!

> Jesus, I give Thee my heart today!
> Jesus, I'll follow Thee all the way,
> Gladly obeying Thee! I will say:
> This I will do with - for Jesus!

About the Author

James Perry has served the Church with more than 54 years of continuous ministry. He attended Columbia Bible College (now Columbia International University) for three years; transferring to Covenant College, a new Presbyterian College in St. Louis, MO from which he graduated with a B.A. in Philosophy. After graduation, he enrolled in Covenant Theological Seminary where he received a B.D. in theology, and returned later for his M.A. He and his wife make their home in Centreville, AL; He has four children; 16 Grandchildren and 14 Great Grandchildren. His other books are available on Amazon.

Realizing Significance, 236 pages, The author summarizes the heart of this book. He explains: "We know about their existence (little people) and some of their needs but we can be so focused on "us", "me", or "I" that we miss seeing or caring for "them", "they" or the "unknown".

Taking A Serious God Seriously, 224 pages, is a clarion call for Christians to return to the standards of Scripture, because God is serious about how Christians should think and live in this world. Every chapter defines what it means to have a serious relationship with a serious God.

The Twenty First Century Church: Is It Waxing Or Waning, 226 pages, This book examines the contemporary church to see if it measures up to the standards of the Bible. It reveals the failure of the church in relationship to the biblical model.

Practical Awareness of Living in the Presence of God, 186 pages, The author wrote this book to give Christians a greater awareness of the Glory of the Lord's Presence in their daily walk and relationship with Him.

Amid the Cultural Chaos: Are We Casualties or Conquerors? 241 pages, Each chapter in this book throws out the gauntlet for Christians to choose a godly culture.

Trending Toward Cultural Captivity: Learning to Survive the Inevitable, 158 pages, This book examines some of the trends that have become overwhelming and a strong influence upon the direction of the nation and world.

Navigating the Cultural Maze: Searching for the Only Way Out, 147 pages, This book will provide you with challenging insights and encouragement to be a light shining into and piercing the darkness in your life.

The Right Course and the Only Right Choice, 154 pages, This book will help Christians gain greater insight in terms of their spiritual journey

The Journey Along the Narrow Way: Jesus Led Me All the Way, 346 pages,

www.ingramcontent.com/pod-product-compliance
Lightning Source LLC
Chambersburg PA
CBHW060830050426
42453CB00008B/637